Walking in *His* Footsteps

A Devotional Journey in the Land of Jesus

MAJOR A. STEWART

WESTBOW°
PRESS
A DIVISION OF THOMAS NELSON
& ZONDERVAN

Author Photograph by Walter Watt

WestBow Press books may be ordered through booksellers or by contacting:

WestBow Press
A Division of Thomas Nelson & Zondervan
1663 Liberty Drive
Bloomington, IN 47403
www.westbowpress.com
1 (866) 928-1240

ISBN: 978-1-4908-8562-9 (sc)
ISBN: 978-1-4908-8563-6 (hc)
ISBN: 978-1-4908-8561-2 (e)

Library of Congress Control Number: 2015909944

Print information available on the last page.

WestBow Press rev. date: 7/24/2015

Praise For

Walking in His Footsteps: A Devotional Journey in the Land of Jesus

What a phenomenal exhortation to walk in the footsteps of Jesus. Dr. Stewart takes his readers on a journey that allows them to identify not only with him, but with Christ. Through his transparency about a once-diminished walk with Christ, Dr. Stewart elegantly details how sometimes the cares of this world can enfeeble our faith. However, through this personal journey in the land of Jesus, even as Jesus was resurrected, Dr. Stewart's faith and commitment to Christ was restored.

Pastor Karen Fikes
Releasing the Fire Kingdom International Ministries, Nashville, TN
Author of *Pushed Into Position*

Walking in His Footsteps is an example of why Rev. Dr. Major A. Stewart is a prolific leader. Dr. Stewart leads one out of the wilderness of darkness, confusion, trials, and life issues into the marvelous light of revelation through his unique perspective gained by walking in the land of Jesus. It is impressive how Dr. Stewart humbly imitates our Savior by reflecting, meditating, praying, and being alone with God, the Father. The fruit of his labor is evident as he allows the reader to experience the *transforming power* of Jesus that will catapult readers into their rightful position to operate in the Lord's kingdom. Excellent work, my son!

Bishop Broderick Huggins
Senior Pastor, St. Paul Baptist Church, Oxnard, CA
President, St. Paul Seminary and Bible Institute, Oxnard, CA
Author of *Cremation from God's View*

In *Walking in His Footsteps*, Dr. Stewart outlines the greatest gift one person can give to another: an introduction to God. In this book, I can feel an outstanding personality shaped by God. In a time when many Christian leaders deal with the stress of life and those in their care, it was refreshing to see how the Lord blessed many but particularly Dr. Stewart with a trip to Israel, the Holy Land, to take time to reflect, renew, reposition, and become restored in his personal walk. After reading this book, I am a believer that God prepares and then uses us to fulfill his purpose!

Tyrone Michael Jordan
Founder and CEO, Jordan & Jordan 3-Strategic Advisors
Clarkston, MI

Dr. Major Adam Stewart has written a book that touches at the heart of why many pastors feel a tremendous burden in ministry; and why there is such a need for reflection, renewal, and ultimately revival. This is a very transparent and transformative piece not just for pastors, but for laborers in the gospel who find that the Lord is transitioning them to a different place in the ministry of Jesus Christ! What a remarkable work!

Rev. Jeffery A. Lang, MA, DD,
President, Michigan Theological Institute, Jackson, MI
Pastor, Southside Church, Jackson, MI

Life is a continual journey full of teachable moments, if we pause to reflect and grow. Sadly, we often fail to notice life's lessons because we hastily rush through experiences to the next encounter without reflection. Dr. Major A. Stewart's *Walking in His Footsteps: A Devotional Journey in the Land of Jesus* presents examples, questions, and exercises that stimulate thought and cultivate spiritual reflection. This book assists the reader in navigating through despair, frustration, and anxiety by tracing the steps of Jesus.

Rev. Dr. Lloyd T. McGriff, Senior Pastor
Galilee Baptist Church, Suitland, MD (*Campus 1*)
Galilee Baptist Church, SE Washington, DC (*Campus 2*)
Author of *Aaron: Mt. Olive's Mouthpiece*

Walking In His Footsteps simply guides you to understand the purpose of the birth, the life, and the resurrection of Christ Jesus through Dr. Stewart's unique revelations as he visited some of the area's most read about in the Holy Bible.

Rev. Terry Randolph, Senior Pastor
Gethsemane Baptist Church
Flint, MI

By choice or force, everyone embarks upon a personal spiritual journey. Typically it is characterized by self-imposed isolation and constant challenges. We often stumble in the dark like children, arriving at our destination bruised or broken. Thanks to Dr. Major Stewart, the journey just got easier! This incredible book provides an intimate look into the personal spiritual journey of Dr. Stewart and guides us to and through our own. You will be generously blessed by every life-changing devotional in this book.

Dr. Leonard N. Smith
Chancellor, Richmond Virginia Seminary
Global Leader of Pastors, Global United Fellowship
Senior Minister, Mount Zion Baptist Church of Arlington, VA
Author of *We Need to Talk: Saying What We Need to Say Without Hurting Each Other*

Dr. Stewart has shown great candor and humility. The Lord allowed me to vicariously see, through Dr. Stewart, where He lay and arose. I could feel the walls of the tomb. I praise God that He has used Dr. Stewart to allow someone like me, who may never visit the Holy Land physically, to see it and feel the experience.

Minister Mary L. Townsend
Corinthians Baptist Church
Muskegon, MI

The Rev. Dr. Major A. Stewart has given us a brilliant bit of meditational literature that promises to provoke the minds and stir the souls of scholars and laity alike. Major Stewart brilliantly applies the Scriptures in a contemporary way. His gift as a writer enables us to experience the Spirit of the land known as holy in a new and unique way.

Rev. Dr. Kim Yarber
Pastor of Mt. Hermon Baptist Church, Flint, MI
President of Great Lakes District Baptist Leadership and Educational Congress
Flint, MI

CONTENTS

I dedicate this book to the following deceased individuals for their loyal support and endless encouragement in the life of this preacher.

- to the late Annie Mae Vaughn-Stewart, who mothered me from her womb to her grave. Annie Mae taught me the value of prayer. She was and is my quiet inspiration. Thank you, "Mama."
- to the late Ruby Dale Fletcher, who also nursed me from a child. As my other mother, she treated me as her own birth child. She believed in me. She called me "Man."
- to the late Luberta Hendricks, my aunt, who took me to church, introducing me to Jesus Christ. In high school, she sometimes cooked me huge pancakes to help cheer me on after the loss of a football game. She always had godly advice for me.
- to the late John Wesley Hendricks, who was my uncle but also a father to me. For many years, he was the family's only source of transportation. He was extremely dependable.
- to the late Albert Stewart, who never treated me any differently than his son. He gave me his last name. What a man!
- to the late Bertha Townsend, who adopted and treated me as one of her own children. The Townsend home was always open to me and the crew—always.
- to the late Frederick "Ricky" Stewart, who was more than my nephew. He was my brother. We traveled the country together. He was my personal confidant. He knew everything about me and still liked me.
- to the late Bill "Cooley" Cowherd, who was a friend when I was friendless.
- to Mr. Henry Harden, who was the kindest and most gentle man I have ever known. I thank him for always giving me an extra slice of bologna when Mother Harden was not looking.

- to the late Rev. John Barnes, who was my high school football defensive coach. He taught me how to defend anybody—I mean, anybody!
- to the late Rev. Lovejoy Johnson Sr., who fathered this preacher for a season in Detroit, Michigan.
- to the late Rev. Gregory Kirksey, who was a friend, brother, and pastor to me. He treated me as his very own son. He introduced me to the art of loving the people of God.
- to the late Rev. Audrian King, who adopted me as his spiritual son and allowed me to practice the art of preaching on the flock under his leadership.
- to the late Rev. Thurman Hargrove, who taught me how to be "instant" in my preaching.
- to the late Rev. Dr. Charles Walker, who always had time to share fatherly advice to a young and inexperienced son. He taught me the art of preaching. He gave me the confidence to write.
- to the late Deacon Bennie Scales and Mother Emma Scales, who always supported me as a young, inexperienced pastor. They taught me the power of unconditional love and support.
- to the late Deacon Howard Keels, who was a great source of encouragement to me during my early years as pastor at Mt. Olive Baptist Church. He taught me the power of making peace.
- to my siblings who are now living on the other side of the Jordan River of Glory, whom I miss so very much:

  • Carrie Johnson-Griffin—She was so pretty and caring.
  • Lottie Mae Stewart—She was a lover of jazz and education.
  • Christine Fletcher—She was my personal protector. And braided my hair!
  • James Wayne Rogers—The very first time I met Wayne, as a youth, I knew he was my big brother.

- James Howard Fletcher—He taught me how to drive a Lincoln, the lean and all.
- Jim "Sonny" Johnson—He taught me never to leave food in the refrigerator without my name on it.

FOREWORD

REV. CLIFTON DAVIS

(Preacher, Actor, Songwriter, Singer, and Host of
Praise the Lord on Trinity Broadcasting Network)

A journey to Jerusalem, in and of itself, is a tremendously stimulating
prospect. All my life, the mere thought or suggestion of travel has
filled me with excitement. A journey to new destinations represents
the promise of adventure, discovery, growth, and learning. As an
enhancement, the possibility of traveling to foreign countries with
fascinating cultures, history, and languages has always taken my
sense of anticipation to an even higher level. God has blessed me to
have visited many countries around the world. But no journey has
touched my life more or had a greater impact on my spiritual being
than a trip to the Holy Land.

*Walking in His Footsteps: A Devotional Journey in the Land of
Jesus* chronicles in a unique way such a pilgrimage undertaken by
its author, Rev. Dr. Major Adam Stewart. Millions have walked in
the footsteps of Jesus, and I am certain many have been inspired or
moved by the experience. But a far smaller number have articulated
that experience with such scholarly and pastoral wisdom. Pastor
Stewart invites the reader to join him from two perspectives: to
accompany him on his personal pilgrimage, lost luggage and all; and

to plumb the depths of our personal spiritual experience by allowing his divinely inspired insights to touch our hearts.

From his experiences at the Mount of Beatitudes to the garden of Gethsemane, God has given Dr. Stewart an anointing that inspired him and compelled him to share deep spiritual insights. He takes us along on the Sea of Galilee, which played a key role in the lives of Jesus and the disciples. Certainly, after walking on the Via Dolorosa (Way of Suffering), the empty tomb ignites a fire of faith when a believer considers that our Savior rose from the dead and walked out of that tomb alive forevermore. Dr. Stewart brings the reader along as he walks in the footsteps of Jesus.

Major A. Stewart clearly has a pastor's heart and a powerful fundamental faith. His education and experience are evident in his writing skills as well as his approachable and practical style. As such, his devotionals can be received in several ways. For the average reader, a few morsels every day can feed the individual's need for biblical insight and spiritual enrichment. "But the word of the LORD was unto them precept upon precept, precept upon precept; line upon line, line upon line; here a little, and there a little" (Isa. 28:13)

However, for the student, Pastor Stewart has provided a valuable resource for examining elements of the steps of Christ through the Holy Land. Additionally, for the pastor, the author has provided sermonic material that can be utilized for homily preparation and for the ongoing propagation of the gospel. Questions are also provided at the end of each chapter to further engage the reader and encourage continued meditation on the thoughts expressed and the Word of God. In whichever aspect one chooses, this book will bless the reader.

Among those chapters that have been of particular edification to me is chapter 8: "What the Storms of Life Can Teach Us." Pastor Stewart guides us to see storms differently; to know that Jesus comes to us in storms, Jesus reveals himself to us in storms, Jesus increases our faith in storms, and Jesus is in charge of storms. Praise God! If you find the outline to be a blessing, read the chapter and get a full serving of this spiritual feast.

I came to know Rev. Dr. Stewart at the recommendation of Rev. Dr. Lloyd McGriff, senior pastor of Galilee Baptist Church, Suitland, Maryland, and subsequently accepted an invitation to minister at Mount Olive Missionary Baptist Church, Flint, Michigan. I found him to be genuine brother in Christ and an extremely gracious host. One of the most obvious characteristics he displayed was his love for God, his family, and his congregation. As I observed his ministry, I was moved to invite him to be my guest on the *Praise the Lord* program on Trinity Broadcasting Network. He was a wonderful guest, and his interview has been viewed hundreds of times.

I heartily recommend adding *Walking in His Footsteps: A Devotional Journey in the Land of Jesus* to your spiritual reading library. It is a gift that will pay life-changing and spirit-filled dividends for years to come.

Clifton Davis, DMin, DLitt

A NOTE FROM REV. RODNEY (HOT ROD) WEDLAW

THE MAN WHO INTRODUCED THE AUTHOR TO JESUS CHRIST

When I select a book for purchase, one of the following three things has happened: the title and purpose of the book captured my attention; the author's story (as told in a foreword, preface, or introduction) has moved me; or it was strongly recommended. In the case of *Walking In His Footsteps: A Devotional Journey in the Land of Jesus*, all three things happened.

When I was approached by Dr. Major A. Stewart to be a contributor to this book, I was honored yet nervous to be considered for such a privilege. It was my intention to share about the man, but knowing he followed the leading of the Holy Spirit, I also desired to give God glory for the man of God He raised up for these end times. I labored day and night while praying for divine direction to share something that would not only acknowledge Dr. Stewart for all the years of brotherhood, of friendship, and of his anointing to be a vessel chosen by God, but to convey to the reader, upon completing these pages, how they will experience the way the power of God can impact one's life. Most importantly, God's grace and mercy are extended to all of his children, as Dr. Stewart witnessed in a few places during his pilgrimage. I suggest the reader look at this personal but spiritually revealing story expecting to grow in Christ! All, from the new convert to the most seasoned Christian, will be motivated to take a spiritual inventory of themselves and seek a more intimate relationship with the Father.

In the book of Jeremiah, chapter 29, verse 11, it is stated God has plans for our lives. Two occasions came to mind as I pondered the forty-plus years Dr. Stewart and I have known each other. These occasions caused me to realize he is in fact walking out the life God destined for Major A. Stewart. The first was in 1973. He and I, along with many of the children in the neighborhood, were ministered to by a group of missionaries. They invited us to come to a Bible study held at their church two days a week. The ministry sent a big gigantic bus to pick us up. At first, we all went just for the candy, but unbeknownst to us, it was a setup for an appointment with our Lord and Savior, Jesus the Christ. On August 22, 1973, I asked Jesus Christ to come into my life. In December of the same year, I introduced Dr. Major A. Stewart to Jesus Christ. That very day, he accepted Jesus Christ as the Lord of his life. My journey took a detour when I became addicted to substances and developed a criminal record that led to jail, then prison. Dr. Stewart stayed on course, and even to this very day has not missed a beat with Christ.

The other occasion that came across my mind was report card day. While attending W. B. Steele Junior High in our hometown of Muskegon, Michigan, I most dreaded report card days because, instead of getting our report cards to take home, as we did in elementary school, the cards were sent by mail. I hurried home with the hope of beating the mailman to my house to intercept the dreaded report card. Needless to say, I missed the mail run, and there was my mother with the report card in hand.

Next the lecture came, accompanied by a beat down, because in our home and neighborhood, education was a priority, and it was enforced in more ways than one. After I was able to gather myself and walk again (it still hurts forty years later), I went down the street to Dr. Stewart's home. He had his report card, and just as we shared the good, we shared the bad. When I saw Major's report card with *all* As, my inquiring mind asked Major how he got such an excellent report card. Major proclaimed to me, "I made it myself." I could have shouted "*Glory!*" from the rooftops. My best friend had made a report card for himself with all As, and surely he would make me one too!

Yet, when I inquired further about how he made it, his reply was, "Hot Rod (which was and still is to this day my nickname), I made this by going to school every day, studying, and doing all my homework." Certainly, that answer was not what I wanted to hear. Even through all these years, Dr. Stewart has continued his pursuit of higher education. One of the happiest days in my life was watching him receive his doctoral degree.

Lastly, I must share the beginning of what came to fruition in this book. I vividly recall one conversation about what would be a dream destination for each of us. I proudly said, "Hawaii, for the pineapples and warm weather!"

When it was Major's turn to share, he said, "I want to go to Israel."

My response was, "Israel?" Curious to hear his reasons, I next asked why.

Major said, "I want to see the place where Jesus was born. I want to walk down the same steps He walked. I want to see the Sea of Galilee, where He performed some of his greatest miracles. I want to see that empty tomb He got up from."

I am so delighted that God provided Dr. Stewart the desire of his heart to go to the Promised Land. I would like to encourage those of you reading this book to step out of the box of your own mind and get into the mind-set of the author as he takes you through a dream that was made real. Dr. Stewart's insight is astounding, due to his studying the Word of God and seeking an education that was pleasing to God. He opened his heart and mind to accept lessons from God during this pilgrimage, which impacted his life and will do the same for you. I promise you that if you read this book, you will receive a blessing from one of the greatest men I have ever met, in the form of Rev. Dr. Major A. Stewart.

Humbly Submitted,
Reverend Rodney G. Wedlaw

Acknowledgments

I would like to thank the following individuals for their loyal support and endless encouragement in the development of this project.

- to my wife, Carla, and lovely daughters, Alexandria, Mikaela, and Karissa for their prayers, support, patience, and unconditional love.
- to my father, Jessie York Sr., who continuously offers his support. Thank you for dropping me off at Eastern Michigan University in September 1979. You gave me life-saving advice: "Son, don't hang around the wrong crowd." I listened to your advice most of the time.
- to my fellow pilgrim teammates, the 2009 Holy Land Pastoral Renewal Team, who willingly ministered to me, as well as one another, prior to, during, and after our journey to Israel. I thank them for their dedication, patience, and wisdom. (The complete list of names is in the appendix.)
- to an awesome leadership team, Jim and Pat Eller, trip coordinator and spiritual director respectively, who lovingly challenged us to see beyond the physical sites to the spiritual meaning.
- to my Mt. Olive Missionary Baptist Church family, who continuously and lovingly encourages their pastor to grow

from glory to glory. Thank you for loving me and my family to life.

- to the Pastoral Search Ministry team members who labored many months in the pastoral search process at Mt. Olive Baptist Church. Thank you for allowing God to use you and your gifts of discernment and leadership.
- to my Gethsemane Missionary Baptist Church family, who prayerfully and financially supported me during this life-changing journey. A special shout out goes to the Pastor's Aid Ministry, under the leadership of Mother Emma Scales (now in glory!).
- to Rafi Muhammad, who has been a friend and a brother through thick and thin times. Even though times have changed, your friendship, love, and support remain constant.
- to my friend and mentor, Rev. Dr. Lloyd T. McGriff, who challenged me beyond my own assessment. Dr. McGriff has encouraged me to pursue excellence continually.
- to my friend and editor, Pastor Jeffery Lang, who grammatically challenged this preacher during struggling moments. I thank him for his scholarly advice and godly wisdom. Pastor Lang has urged me to the finish line.
- to Deacon Harold and Mrs. Iphagenia Brooks, my parent-in-laws. I thank them for their unending support toward worthwhile endeavors. And spoiling me as their only son-in-law.
- to Mrs. Minnie Harden, my godmother and my personal Bible instructor. She consistently encouraged me during the early years of ministry development.
- to Sharon Granberry-Campbell, an author and coworker, who encouraged me over the years to write.
- to Lenoral Lee, a friend who possesses the gift of encouragement. You have encouraged me beyond measure to write until I finished. Thank you.

- to Wanda Brown, who has the gift of good taste and willingly gave good advice on cover and picture matters.
- to Troy Brown, who has been a major source of encouragement from the very first day I met him. His brotherhood and encouragement continues to be the Mt. Olive oil that refreshes my spirit as I continue the journey.
- to my "Sands," the honorable men of Alpha Phi Alpha, Epsilon Eta Chapter, FOT (Fusion of Tenacity), Eastern Michigan University: Tommy (Diane) Dickerson; William (Priscilla) Huddleston Sr.; Edgar (Patricia) Kennebrew Sr.; Duane (Regina) Haywood; Tony Way; and Tyrone (Sherri) Jordan Sr. Thank you for pushing me!
- to my niece Nikki Hutcherson, who would not let me forget the importance of finishing what God has started.
- to my executive assistants, former and present: Doris Smiley (former), Margaret Wren (former), and Renita Bingham (present). Thank you for your continued inspiration, support, and encouragement to write until finished.
- to Rev. Lovejoy Johnson, who has always given me his support in every worthwhile endeavor. He has encouraged me to write at my best.
- to my godsister Kimberly Davis and daughter Tiffany Fife, who have always encouraged me to be the best me I could be. I thank them for their love and encouragement.
- to Mr. James Rowan, who encouraged me to read fully, speak readily, and write exactly. He taught me the value of investing in those whom you love.
- to Rev. Moses Bingham, my youth pastor and one of my sons in the ministry, who willingly offered fresh ideas for writing successfully.
- to my virtual assistant and project manager, Yolanda Black, who encouraged the writer to dare be what God has ordained him to be. Thank you!

- to my brilliant and blessed godchildren, Kamilah Griffith, Carla Kirksey, Na'imah Muhammad, Tyrone Jordan II, and Evan C. Kennebrew. I give God praise and glory for who you are yet becoming. You inspire me!
- to Elder James Larry, who took me in under his guidance as a new-hire GM college graduate. He treated me as his own little brother with love, protection, and prayer.
- to Pastor Frederick Flowers, who lovingly challenged me to grow and develop as a responsible preacher. Pastor Flowers taught me the value of being faithful.
- to Bishop Broderick Huggins, who ordained and further prepared me for ministry. He taught me the importance of staying ready to preach the gospel.
- to Dr. Darrell Gilyard, who challenged me, loved me, encouraged me, and demanded excellence from me.
- to Rev. Seldon Williams, who has been a brother and mentor to me during times of difficulty. Thank you for helping me to see the way.
- to Bishop Rory Cavette, who has always been a strong supporter and encourager of my ministry
- to Minister Laura Carpenter-Pritchard, who has been a source of strength since we were both tenth graders in high school. Thank you for your continued support in ministry.
- to Pastor Marvin Jennings, who willingly shared with me valuable resources that resulted in this manuscript. He taught me the value of being unselfish in ministry.
- to Rev. Dr. Roosevelt Austin, who wrote a profound afterword. You are simply a gift from God! Thank you for sharing your gift of pastoring to all who will follow.
- to Rev. Dr. Clifton Davis, who wrote a masterful foreword. Thank you for sharing your gifts of preaching, singing, acting, and songwriting with the world. Because of you, the world is blessed by "Never Can Say Goodbye."

- to Deacon Kevin Hatchett, who spent untold hours serving as a personal assistant as I served from another city and state. I thank you for your faithfulness and friendship.
- to Brother Walter Watt, who is a brother from my hood and fraternity. Thank you for taking time to help make me look good with your photography skills.
- to the following persons who took time to read and critique the manuscript with great care: Ann McCloud, Betty Tipper, and Melva Viltz. Thank you for being used by God to help guide and challenge the thoughts of this author.
- to the New Life Chapel Missionaries, who saw in me what God saw in me. Thank each of you for pouring into me, and others, the love and Word of God: Rev. and Mrs, Washburn, Rev. and Mrs. Jim Lash, Rev. and Mrs. Luke Wilson, and many others. Thank you!
- to all my wonderful *living* siblings, who are the best group of brothers and sisters any one person can have. Each of them have inspired me in such great ways. In age order:

  - Robert Fletcher—When I had hair, you kept it cut! Never charged me a penny!
  - Thomas Stewart—You saved my life!
  - Merlean Fletcher—You are responsible for my superior typing skills. You gave me my first typewriter as a high school graduation gift.
  - Rosemary Stewart—You remind me so much of Momma.
  - Melvin Fletcher—You are the reason why I was not afraid of bullies in school. I remember when you dethroned Billy Ray and became the "king" of Angel Elementary!
  - Alvin Fletcher—You are a gentle giant of a man who is extremely protective of your family … all of us! You have stood up for me more than once!

- Valerie Hough—You are such a kind soul of a woman.
- Jessie Mae Watkins—Even though you are my baby sister, more and more you are like another mother to me. I love you for that.
- Thurnell (Buddy) Stewart—There is no one like you! I love you, man! Everybody loves Buddy!
- Jessie York Jr.—I am so proud of the man you have become. You are a brilliant brother!

- to all my wonderful nephews, nieces, and cousins! You all know there's too many of you to start writing names. In part, my inspiration for writing is because of you. I want you to know who Uncle Major is, but more importantly, I want you to know who Jesus is.
- to a countless number of others whose names are too many to call, I say to you, "Thank you!"

Introduction

What an Opportunity

On Thursday, August 27, 2009, I reported to Mitchell International Airport in Milwaukee, Wisconsin, to take a flight to Tel Aviv and begin the journey of a lifetime—to walk where Jesus walked. I, along with twenty other pastors from across the country was invited, all expenses paid, by the United Theological Seminary of Dayton, Ohio, on a two-week pastoral sabbath and renewal trip. This journey was funded through a generous grant from the Cousins Foundation. Additionally, we were blessed to have Pat Eller, spiritual director, and James (Jim) Eller, trip coordinator, to be our team guides for the entire trip.

As I reflected on my life-changing experience of walking where Jesus walked in the Holy Land, I began to see God and His Word in an entirely different light. I encountered many life-changing experiences, *some* of which I will share in this writing. I suppose that if I shared all or even most of my experiences, I would be typing for the balance of my life here on earth. Thus, I will attempt to share only those experiences that will challenge and encourage the reader to walk more closely, more enthusiastically, and more transparently in His steps.

The happenstances discussed in this book are not necessarily unique to me. I am reasonably confident that these encounters have been experienced by many others who have gone before me. But these are unique inasmuch as they were birthed from my spiritual womb. Reverend Carey Brassfield, an associate minister at our church, is an identical twin. Rev. Brassfield informed me that, even though they look identical to the outside world, he and his brother are yet unique, one from another. Thus, even though other pilgrims have walked in His steps in the Holy Land, my encounters and my experiences are nevertheless unique.

FROM OPPORTUNITY TO REALITY

I am thankful and blessed to have been one of the few selected to participate in this most worthy experience. Sometime during the first quarter of 2009, I received an e-mail from United Theological Seminary (UTS), from which I graduated as a doctoral student. The e-mail invited me to apply for a grant to travel to Israel for the Israel Pilgrimage.

Now, to begin, there were thousands of qualified UTS graduates who could have been selected to represent such a prodigious school of theological thought. I wondered what made me so unique that I would even be given consideration in a pool of so many more qualified candidates? I was one of eighty pastors to apply for the grant and was blessed to be one of twenty selected to participate.

Each pilgrim, including the spiritual director and trip coordinator, was used by God to minister to and encourage me in a profound way. Peter says, "Like good stewards of the manifold grace of God, serve one another with whatever gift each of you has received. For this, I am eternally grateful for the experience" (1 Pet. 4:10 NRSV). During the course of the pilgrimage, we had many opportunities to minister to one another, both personally as well as in group form. My most memorable interactions with these ministers of God was how they each used their unique spiritual giftings to minister to me, a wandering sheep of a preacher/pastor while on the pilgrimage. What an amazing group of Christian men and women.

A REQUIRED RESPONSE TO HIS GRACE

The Scripture bears witness that "for unto whomsoever much is given, of him shall be much required: and to whom men have committed much, of him they will ask the more" (Luke 12:48b). My response to the grace given to me through this pilgrimage experience is a written reflection of my journey in the Holy Land.

The pilgrimage challenged, changed, and strengthened my spiritual life in a number of ways. First, it allowed me to experience the birthplace of my faith. It helped me affirm the reality of what my faith means in my life. I am a believer in Jesus Christ, and I am thankful for what He accomplished through His atonement. However, experiencing the pilgrimage has mightily impacted and affirmed my personal belief system in ways that reading, studying, and living had been unable to do.

Additionally, this experience allowed me to "see" the Word of God come alive in a way afforded to very few people. There is an exceptional feeling that can be experienced when sailing on the Sea of Galilee and walking the streets of the Via Dolorosa, as did Jesus. There is something amazing about physically going into the Jesus tomb and seeing for oneself that the tomb is empty! Turning to exit the empty tomb, there is a signpost that reads "He is not here, for He is risen." When my natural eyes lay hold of that signage for the very first time, it brought me to my knees, in tears, with thanksgiving in my heart. It instantly furthered a profound change of heart and spirit within my already happy soul.

From this experience, God's Word became clearer, my faith became deeper, and my passion for Christ and ministry became stronger than when I began the journey. While I was in Galilee, each day was filled with prayer, excursions, worship, reflection, and plenty of native foods. We visited sites such as the Mount of Beatitudes; Cliff Arbel; Capernaum, where Jesus headquartered His ministry; Tabgha, where Jesus fed the five thousand with two fish and five loaves; the Chapel of the Primacy of Peter, where Jesus appeared to the disciples while they were fishing; the Sea of Galilee, where Jesus announced "Peace, be still"; Ein Gev and Kursi, where Jesus healed the demoniac and cast the demons into swine; Sepphoris, where Jesus probably worked during the day with his father, Joseph; Nazareth, where Jesus grew up; Mount Tabor, where the transfiguration took place; Banis or Caesarea Philippi, where Jesus posed the question to His disciples, "Whom do men say that I am?"; and the foot of Mount Hermon, where the Jordan River originates from springs feeding small streams.

While in Jerusalem, we visited sites such as Megiddo (Armageddon), where Josiah met his death in a struggle with Pharaoh, 2 Kings 23:28–30; Caesarea Maritime, where Peter preached the gospel to Cornelius, a Roman centurion, in Acts 10, and Paul was imprisoned before being sent to Rome, Acts 23:23–26; the Mount of Olives and the garden of Gethsemane, where Jesus prayed in agony and was betrayed by Judas; Via Dolorosa and the Church of the Holy Sepulchre, the various stations of Jesus's route to die on the cross); the Garden of the Tomb of Jesus; the Wailing Wall; the upper room; Bethlehem, Jesus's birth home; the Dead Sea; the Masada, a fortress of Herod; Qumran, where the Dead Sea Scrolls were found; and Jericho.

WHY YOU SHOULD READ THIS BOOK

Over a period of years, as the Lord has given me inspiration and opportunity to work on this manuscript, I discovered each time I picked up my pen to write, I was at a different place on my spiritual journey. As I wrote about daily excursions and reflections of our pilgrimage, I saw with a different set of eyes each time I picked up my proverbial pen. I did not write from the opinion of a political analyst of any sort, even though there were many political events going on during my short stay in Jerusalem. The scope of this manuscript was only from the spiritual vantage point of walking where Jesus walked.

As you read what I have written, my deepest desire is for you to reflect upon your own spiritual journey and ultimately experience a changed life from interacting with this book. For those of you who have yet to travel to the Holy Land and experience firsthand what I have written about, I pray that you will at least be spiritually challenged to enjoy an even deeper walk with the Lord. For those of you who have already been to the Holy Land at some time in the past, my prayer for you is a renewed sense of experience as you draw upon your reflections and previous encounters with walking where Jesus walked.

In any case, my ultimate prayer is each time you pick up this book and read it, a life-changing experience will result. My desire is that every time you open your Bible for the remainder of your life, you will have a picture in your mind of the sacred places written about in this book. My prayer is that the pages of the Bible will go from being black and white to living color in your mind. My prayer is that each reader who dares to walk where Jesus walked will "see" where He died for our sins and "see" where He rose from the dead with the sovereignty of power and might. My prayer is that you will never be the same again.

Soli Deo Gloria!

A NOTE ON THE FORMAT OF THIS BOOK

Each chapter of this devotional journey starts by briefly reviewing the day's excursions in chronological order (to the best of my memory). Unfortunately, I was unable to give equal writing attention to each location. I have not written in detail about every place we visited, though I mention most of them. As I reflect on each day's experience, I am careful to mention my personal encounters with the various sites. I attempted to write about my own struggles as I tried to find balance within my spiritual walk with the Lord during that time in my life.

There is also an attempt to discuss briefly both the biblical and historical influences on the various sites, where I thought such discussion most appropriate. Additionally, each chapter includes a devotional Scripture passage that was assigned by the spiritual director and group leader for that day, based upon the various sites visited. Each devotional passage is expounded upon in an effort to inspire the reader to dare indeed walk or continue to walk more closely with Jesus.

Some of the devotions are original. Some of them are rewritten from sermons I have preached at some point in the past. Some were birthed from experiences since my journey to the land of Jesus. Some of them are a hybrid of original sermon material I have preached, sermon material of others, and sermon material from my own experiences. My goal is to engage the reader to experience the journey as I did.

Finally, each chapter concludes with questions for further discussion and reflection. They are designed to provoke a closer examination of one's life journey as one reflectively walks in the footsteps of Jesus. It is my hope that this format allows for individuals or small groups to encounter a spiritual awakening or reawakening, as the case may be, while simultaneously receiving inspiration to develop a deeper and more meaningful relationship with Jesus Christ.

Chapter 1

THE ABSENTEEISM OF JESUS

*Day 1, Thursday, August 27, 2009: Milwaukee,
WI; Dayton, OH; Houston, TX*

BEGINNING THE PILGRIMAGE

A pilgrim is a person who journeys, usually long distance, to some sacred place as an act of religious devotion. The journey itself is described as a *pilgrimage*. On Thursday, August 27, 2009, I started on my pilgrimage to the Holy Land, thanks to the Cousins Foundation. I was not going on a vacation or as a tourist. The purpose of my pilgrimage was to detach, renew, refresh, and refocus. I wanted to detach from the routines of life as a bivocational pastor and a district sales manager for General Motors (GM). I needed to get clarity, renewal, refreshment, and focus on the mission that God has preordained for my life and ministry. I needed a rekindling of the spirit.

Airport Fellowship

One of the things that made the pilgrimage to Israel so memorable and life-changing was how God used this trip to confront many of the personal problems and issues I was facing. My state of mind was one of doubt and uncertainty.

I was doubtful about my future as a GM employee. GM was downsizing its sales force, and my position as district sales manager was likely to be one of the job assignments downsized. Of course, I was deeply concerned about possibly losing my job or moving to another territory, farther away from Gethsemane Baptist Church in Flint, Michigan.

Additionally, I was uncertain about my future as the senior pastor of Gethsemane. I was living and working in a different city and state, six hours away (one way, driving) from Gethsemane. The long commute was wearing on my mind and body. I had been commuting for about three years from Waukesha, Wisconsin, to Flint. I was weary and worn. Even though my ministry was very fulfilling where God had planted me, I felt a continual pulling within my heart and mind. I believe that God was even then preparing me for another assignment.

The other area of my struggle was that a new church for which I was a pastoral candidate was located in the city of Flint as well. The overlapping of church memberships was a concern. What do I mean by overlapping church memberships? Members of Gethsemane Baptist Church were either close friends or related in some way to members of Mt. Olive Baptist Church. The black Baptist tradition in Flint does not typically include calling a pastor from a neighboring church. This practice is not new or uncustomary in other denominations, but it seems almost forbidden in some black Baptist church circles. I commend the Mt. Olive Baptist Church for their vision and creativity in allowing me to be one of the candidates for the pastorate at the Mount.

But even as I struggled in these areas, my heart's desire was to be and to live within the will of God. I would rather live at odds with others and be in the will of God than to live peaceably with men and live outside the will of God. Still, I struggled. I understood that pastors do not choose where they pastor; God plants them where He wants them, for they belong to Him and not the church (Jer. 3:15; Eph. 4:11–16; Rev. 1:20). Still, I struggled.

There was also a struggle from within my spiritual journey. While I was personally involved in church and ministry activities, I was not as relationally close to God as I desired. I was sinking; it was as if I was moving around but not moving *in* the things of God. I was living a wilderness experience. I was running in circles but never reaching my destination. Everything as it related to ministry seemed very difficult to accomplish. My prayer life was lacking. My preaching wanted depth, even for me! I was in bad shape.

Many of the Mothers of the church—in the African American Baptist church, they are typically spiritually and chronologically mature women who function as spiritual mothers, nourishing and protecting the believers—were an encouragement to me, even when they sensed my inner struggles during a preaching event. I do not know exactly how they detected my struggles, but I guess the adage "mothers know everything" may also be true of the Mothers of the church. They did not verbalize their knowledge but I knew they sensed something. They would carefully say things like, "Oh, Pastor, you keep on preaching. It's going to get better!" Other times, it was noticeable in the way they held on to my hand and simply said, "Pastor, I am praying for you." I instinctively knew what they were saying. You may say they could read between the lines.

A childhood memory comes to mind. I would sometimes cause Annie Mae, my biological mother, public embarrassment, and she would say, "Boy, when we get home …" She did not have to finish the sentence or provide clarity. There was not a doubt, in my mind or hers, what was on the agenda when we arrived home. Momma often extended grace without saying one word: she would give me the look of ultimatum. Even as a child, I was able to read between those lines, and most of the time, I was right.

The same discernment aided in my understanding of the thoughts, spoken or unspoken, of my spiritual mothers. I knew they were saying, "Son, we are praying for you. We are lifting you up in encouragement, so you might continue doing whatever, stop doing whatever, and start doing whatever you need to in order to draw closer to Jesus!"

The bottom line was, clearly, the influence and power of Jesus were missing in my life. I desperately desired that power to flow through my life again.

A LIFE-SAVING EXPERIENCE

In the handbook *A Pilgrimage to the Holy Land*, an article written by a fellow pilgrim gave me very good insight on what the modern day pilgrimage is all about: "Moses withdrew from the people, climbed the Holy Mountain and engaged in a one-on-one with God." When Elijah felt threatened by Jezebel, he fled to Mount Sinai to talk with God. That same guiding thought inspired early Christian pilgrims to travel to the Holy Land to experience firsthand the land where Jesus had walked and taught, and where the Christian faith was born.

"We modern pilgrims realize how Jesus took time by Himself to pray and to rest with His disciples. He remained focused on the mission that God, His Father, sent Him to do, and repeatedly withdrew to regain inspiration. Pilgrimages can help pastors and leaders see themselves apart from the congregations they lead and be able to assess their strengths and weaknesses, their wisdom and folly."[1]

Looking back, the timing of this pilgrimage was precise and needful. I desperately needed time to withdraw from my congregation, my secular vocation, and other influences to understand better and attend to my personal issues and ministry challenges. Moreover, I needed to regain some inspiration and perspective. My soul required serious time with Jesus. I needed to hear from Jesus, not just when I was preparing a sermon or a Bible study, but during times of personal devotion and reflection.

Little did I know that this pilgrimage was God's prescription for a worsening case of spiritual malnourishment. This pilgrimage was God's lifeline to a preacher who was drowning as surely as the *Titanic*, with no rescue in sight. It was a slow and certain drowning, but I did not want to die. I did not like living below the spiritual poverty level, being a child of the King who owns everything. I wanted not only to survive; I wanted to live victoriously with power and might. I needed to experience the very presence of Jesus again.

Scripture Reflection: Luke 2:41–52 KJV

> Now his parents went to Jerusalem every year at the feast of the Passover. And when he was twelve years old, they went up to Jerusalem after the custom of the feast. And when they had fulfilled the days,

---

[1] Max Miller. *A Pilgrimage to the Holy Land*, Holy Land Pastoral Renewal Program (CF Foundation, 2009),11.

as they returned, the child Jesus tarried behind in Jerusalem; and Joseph and his mother knew not of it. But they, supposing him to have been in the company, went a day's journey; and they sought him among their kinsfolk and acquaintance. And when they found him not, they turned back again to Jerusalem, seeking him. And it came to pass, that after three days they found him in the temple, sitting in the midst of the doctors, both hearing them, and asking them questions. And all that heard him were astonished at his understanding and answers. And when they saw him, they were amazed: and his mother said unto him, Son, why hast thou thus dealt with us? behold, thy father and I have sought thee sorrowing. And he said unto them, How is it that ye sought me? wist ye not that I must be about my Father's business? And they understood not the saying which he spake unto them. And he went down with them, and came to Nazareth, and was subject unto them: but his mother kept all these sayings in her heart. And Jesus increased in wisdom and stature, and in favour with God and man.

THE DEVOTIONAL

In this passage of Scripture, we find Jesus and His parents taking a pilgrimage to Jerusalem. Luke 2:41–42 says, "Every year Jesus' parents went to Jerusalem for the Festival of the Passover. When he was twelve years old, they went up to the festival, according to the custom" (NIV). The Hebrew Scriptures, in three separate places, called for the mandatory attendance of all males age thirteen and above at the feasts of Passover, Pentecost, and Tabernacles (cf. Exod.

23:14–17, 34:23; Deut. 16:16). No such requirement was made of women, though godly women such as Hannah had been attending Passover for centuries (1 Sam. 2:19). Thus, the multiple pilgrimages of Joseph and Mary together testify to their profound devotion and love for God.

Passover had become a family event observed along with others from Nazareth (the word translated "company" in Luke 2:44 was used to describe a traveling party or caravan). The high number of people in the caravan provided safety as they passed through the hostile area of Samaria, and also added to their camaraderie. The psalmist confirms this thought in Ps. 121:1–8.

The lesson here is, as parents, it is essential to establish regular habits of attending worship early in the lives of children. Furthermore, the sense of priority toward worship needs to be demonstrated both at home and by regularly attending church. Clearly, it is more than just about going to church out of habit or because of some family tradition. It is about seeking God for worshipful opportunities because of His goodness and grace. For the Scriptures, declares, "God is spirit, and his worshipers must worship in the Spirit and in truth" (John 4:24).

WHEN WE DISCOVER THE ABSENTEEISM OF JESUS

After the Passover celebration, Joseph and Mary left Jerusalem, but they left without their son, Jesus. The fact that Joseph and Mary were unaware that Jesus was not with them is an incredible thought, from a parent's perspective. You would think, in view of who Jesus is, that His absence would have been very evident to them. Notice the length of time that passed before they noticed the absenteeism of Jesus. It took a whole day for them to realize He was not with them. The spiritual application here is that many people travel many days, years, and sometimes a lifetime without the presence of Jesus in their lives.

When Joseph and Mary realized Jesus was not with them, they began to investigate where He might be. I imagine they first looked among the large group in which they were traveling. Then they probably looked in another group that had kids about the same age as Jesus.

Joseph and Mary were alarmed when they could not find Jesus in the caravan. Eventually, they decided to head back to Jerusalem and see if somehow Jesus had become lost and found his way back to Jerusalem. Going back to Jerusalem meant traveling alone, without the security of the group. Their failure to make sure Jesus was with them caused an inconvenience and a delay in their journey.

Similarly, when the influence and presence of Jesus are absent from our lives, our destinies are often delayed. Simply put, we need the guidance of Jesus to help us travel on the right path and direction. We need His presence to give us confidence that we can do all things through Christ who gives us strength (Phil. 4:13). We need Jesus to walk with us.

When Jesus Is Present

Finally, after three days of searching, Joseph and Mary found Jesus in the temple, amazing and astonishing the leaders. First of all, they found Jesus sitting down. According to the customs of the day, for Jesus to be *sitting* in the midst of the religious teachers was a place of honor, especially for a twelve-year-old boy. I have discovered that Jesus desires to sit on the thrones of our hearts. He wants and deserves to sit there.

Peter declares, "But sanctify Christ as Lord in your hearts, always being ready to make a defense to everyone that asks you to give an account for the hope that is in you, yet with gentleness and reverence" (1 Pet. 3:15). What does it mean to "sanctify Christ as Lord in your hearts"? *Sanctify* means to "hallow" or to "make holy." It should be the aim for every believer in Christ to make a home for Jesus in our hearts.

Some time ago, a preacher friend of mine was the guest preacher at Mt. Olive Baptist Church. He was escorted by one of the associate ministers to the pulpit to be seated. I was already sitting in the pulpit, in the pastor's place. As my guest was being escorted toward me, I stood up, stepping away from my position and inviting the preacher to sit in the pastor's seat. When Jesus is present, we should get out of the way and give Him the place of honor in our hearts.

Don't allow anything or anyone to sit on the throne of your life. Jesus said, "No one can serve two masters; for either he will hate the one and love the other, or he will hold to the one and despise the other. You cannot serve both God and mammon" (Matthew 6:24).

I find it very interesting that, when Joseph and Mary found Jesus, He was engaged in a profound dialogue: listening, asking, and answering questions. Jesus showed proper respect for the elders and teachers by first listening to what they had to say.

It is very difficult to engage in productive and meaningful conversation without listening to what others have to say. It amazes me how some Christian adults find it difficult to sit down and partake in Christian dialogue without respectfully listening to the concerns of others. The pilgrimage also presented an opportunity for meaningful socialization. There was much time to catch up on family happenings such as births, birthdays, deaths, and marriages. This type of socialization helps develop a true spirit of unity, love, and humility. That's why Peter exclaimed, "Finally, all of you, have unity of spirit, sympathy, love for one another, a tender heart, and a humble mind" (1 Pet. 3:8 NRSV).

After Joseph and Mary had found Jesus in the temple, it appears that Mary blamed Jesus for His absence. That's right; they tried to blame Jesus for His absence in their lives. However, it was not the responsibility of the child to keep up with the parents, but rather it was the parents' responsibility to keep up with the child.

Likewise, it is our responsibility to keep Jesus present in our lives on a daily basis. You see, when a person makes the decision to invite Jesus into his or her life, it is important to know that through the Holy Ghost, Jesus is always present. In Revelation 3:20, Jesus makes this offer: "Behold, I stand at the door and knock; if any one hears my voice and opens the door, I will come into him and eat with him, and he with me"(ESV). Now the question is, did you open the door of your heart to the Lord?

Child of God, Jesus is present right now in your life! In John 6:37, Jesus said, "All that the Father gives me will come to me; and him who comes to me I will not cast out" (ESV). In other words, once you make a decision to accept Jesus as your Savior, you belong to God and He will never cast you aside.

In John 10:27–29, Jesus said, "My sheep hear my voice, and I know them, and they follow me; and I give them eternal life, and they shall never perish, and no one shall snatch them out of my hand. My Father, who has given them to me, is greater than all, and no one is able to snatch them out of the Father's hand" (ESV). Wow! Jesus says no one has the authority to remove you from His presence. That's a wonderful thought!

Sometimes the presence of Jesus seems absent in my life. The times when His presence seems most absent are when I allow "things" to distract me, and I fail to spend sufficient quiet time with Him in prayer and Bible study. No one is permanently immune from this unfortunate occurrence. Getting to know Him better requires that I spend time in His Word, as well as asking Him to reveal more of Himself to me (2 Tim. 2:15).

When a guy is interested in a girl beyond friendship, he will typically desire to spend more and more quality time with her. Conversely, if he is no longer attracted to her, his desire to spend time with her begins to wane. The same concept is true in the spiritual life of the believer.

BE ABOUT THE FATHER'S BUSINESS

Jesus responded to His parents, "I must be about my Father's business" (Luke 2:49). Jesus came to earth to do the will of the heavenly Father (Ps. 40:8). In fact, His only desire was to do the will of God.

Obedience to God is not limited to Jesus; it is the business of all God's children. When Jesus said, "I must," he put serving God in the "must" category. Too many of us put serving God in the "I will as long as I get my way" or "I will from time to time" category.

The good news is that when we are continually about our Father's business, we are guaranteed His abiding presence.

> If you abide in me, and my words abide in you, ask whatever you will, and it shall be done for you. By this, my Father is glorified, that you bear much fruit, and so prove to be my disciples. As the Father has loved me, so have I loved you; abide in my love. If you keep my commandments, you will abide in my love, just as I have kept my Father's commandments and abide in his love. These things I have spoken to you, that my joy may be in you, and that your joy may be full. (John 15:7–11)

And as long as we abide in Him, He is never absent from us!

For Further Discussion and Reflection:

1. What kinds of pilgrimages or retreats have you participated in? Which one was most meaningful to you and why?
2. How does the Old Testament passage Psalm 121:1–8 help us better understand the context of a pilgrimage?
3. Has "the presence of Jesus" ever been absent in your life? How?
4. What were the steps you took to reclaim the feeling of His presence in your life?
5. What does it mean to "be about the Father's business"?

Chapter 2

THE MISSION OF THE CHURCH

Day 2, Friday, August 28, 2009: Travel from
the States to Galilee and Tiberias

This pilgrimage journey of a lifetime lasted for two weeks, with half the time spent in Galilee and half in Jerusalem. Each morning through early afternoon, we made excursions to a place or places of biblical interest.

The first day of the trip was spent traveling from the United States. We arrived at the Tel Aviv International Airport in Tel Aviv, Israel, on Friday, August 28, 2009. The lessons I was to learn on the pilgrimage began upon our arrival, when I became aware that my luggage was lost. The realization of the potential loss of many material items of value to me left me devastated at first, but later spiritually enriched. It became prophetically clear my mental transition was as necessary as my physical transition from the United States to the Holy Land.

MY LOST LUGGAGE

As I stretched from the trip, preparing to go through customs, the thought came to mind, "If only Annie Mae and Ruby Dale (my deceased mother and deceased stepmother, respectively) could see me now, they would be as happy as I."

My next thought was to pick up my luggage and make a straight way to a bed. We were all able to directly process through customs to reclaim our luggage. Everything was wonderful until I discovered that everyone had successfully retrieved their luggage except me. After investigating the matter, I found out that my luggage had somehow ended up in Houston, Texas. Now that's a long way away from Israel, no matter how you slice it. The good news was knowing the exact location; the bad news was that no one could tell me with any degree of certainty when or how I was going to get my lost luggage back.

During the following days in Galilee, I regularly contacted the airline to check the status of my luggage. Each time, a representative told me the luggage was still in Houston, waiting for a shipping order to Israel. The most frustration came with the knowledge that both airlines involved were aware of the exact location of my luggage, but no one could seem to resolve the shipping problem! And when I pressed for more information, the customer service representative's attention to my concern was less than acceptable.

Here I was, prepared for the journey of a lifetime, a pilgrimage to discover the core of my spiritual purpose—and I was encountering a distraction. A foreign place, an unfamiliar place, and not one familiar possession of mine were accessible. Nor could I rest peacefully in my most comfortable pajamas!

Eventually, I did receive my luggage. It was nine days later.

Looking back on this experience, God taught me some lessons that were imperative for me to learn.

RECLAIMING GOD'S LOST LUGGAGE

It is the awesome task of the church to get God's lost luggage and return it to its rightful owner—God! Jesus has already filled out the missing luggage claim report and authorized the church to make disciples of everyone, baptizing them in the name of the Father, Son, and Holy Ghost and teaching them to observe and obey every command of God. (Matt. 28:19–20).

Now what the church must do is execute the claim report, get the lost luggage, and take it to the Master.

Jim Eller leading the pilgrims in group discussion

The good news is, we have already identified the location of the lost luggage. We see them at the grocery store, at work, at school, on the basketball court, and in the doctor's office. We see them standing in line at Walmart, and we see them driving down the streets of Flint. Some of us have lost luggage in our homes: sleeping in our beds, eating our food, and sitting on our sofas. Some of them haven't been to church in a very long time. Have we attempted to reach out and reclaim them?

Since we all know where they are, we don't have to wait on the pastor, the evangelism ministry or the mission ministry to retrieve the luggage. Individually, as Christians, we can evangelize and share the good news of Jesus with them. We must be motivated to retrieve them and take them to their rightful Owner.

We are God's luggage. The unfortunate fact is some of God's luggage remains lost. Some of His luggage is misplaced, mistagged, and mishandled. It has been incorrectly checked in to the wrong destination in life. His luggage should be with Him but is sitting in some unknown place, waiting to be reclaimed and taken to its rightful owner, God. And this we must do. We must take it to God, because God so loved the world that He sacrificed His only begotten Son for each piece of luggage.

The Master has need of His luggage. He has need of His luggage because each piece is uniquely extraordinary and eternally valuable to God.

I once read a story about a man who lived in a tiny apartment and died in extreme poverty. At one point in his life, he had even been homeless, living on the streets. He did not have many friends. He never authored a book. He never invented anything. He had no successes to speak of or any noted victories. He was just a poor man who lived and died as another face in the crowd.

After the funeral, some family members went to his little run-down apartment to remove his belongings. They found a painting hanging on the wall and sold it at a garage sale. The woman who bought it took it to a local art gallery for an appraisal and was shocked to discover that the painting was almost priceless. The piece of art that had hung for so many years in a little run-down apartment had been painted by a famous artist who lived in the early 1800s. The woman auctioned off that painting for several million dollars!

Just think how that poor man's life might have changed if he had known the value of what he possessed. How might he have lived if only he had been connected to his true value in life? Think about the many options he had but did not know about because he had not realized his true worth. He was a multimillionaire and didn't even know it!

That's why God wants His luggage reclaimed. There is tremendous eternal value in each piece of luggage. We are of extreme value to God!

Scripture Reflection: Matthew 28:18–20 KJV

And Jesus came and spake unto them, saying, All power is given unto me in heaven and in earth. Go ye therefore, and teach all nations, baptizing them in the name of the Father, and of the Son, and of the Holy Ghost: Teaching them to observe all things whatsoever I have commanded you: and, lo, I am with you alway, even unto the end of the world. Amen.

The Devotional

These were Jesus's parting words to the church just prior to His ascension. It is here that we discover our purpose in life. Matthew 28:18–20 is referred to by many as the mission statement for the church. This Scripture marks out our marching orders. It is our game plan. It is here that Jesus clearly laid out the purpose and plan for the church to continue in His physical, earthly absence.

Sadly, many have ignored the Great Commission. Rather, it has become the Gross Omission. One noted author said,

The emergence of such omission by churches did not begin in our generation, but many down through the ages have failed in their purpose. When the idea of foreign missions was introduced to the Baptist faith, it was met with considerable opposition. Many have trouble following the command of our Lord when it comes to evangelism and missions. Listed are some frightening statistics: 95% of all Christians have never led a person to Christ; 80% of believers have no consistent witness for the Lord; less than 2% are actively involved in some evangelistic ministry;

and 71% give nothing toward financing missions or evangelistic ministries.[2]

These numbers are troubling, but they reveal just where the modern church exists. Christ, by example, set before us the Great Commission as a priority. These were His final instructions for the church. We have work to do, and we can do it!

WE HAVE THE CONFIDENCE OF CHRIST

Jesus said that "all power" in the heavens and the earth is given to Him. This is a significant statement. This verse is important because it gives us the confidence we need on our journey to retrieve God's luggage and take it to Jesus through evangelism. We have received our orders—to reclaim those who are lost without Christ, mistagged and unclaimed—from the One who possesses "all power." This is meaningful for the Christian because the power Jesus possesses is the same power that enables us to carry out His work. With this power, even the "gates of hell" can't stop us, the church, from doing what Jesus has called us to do (Matt. 16:18). We have confidence in accomplishing His will because His power indwells us! We can do all things through Christ who gives us strength (Phil. 4:13).

WE HAVE THE COMMAND OF CHRIST

In Matthew 28:19, the first thing we find Jesus telling us is "Go." This is a word that requires and expects action. Jesus was telling us to get busy, get up, and get going! "*Go* and fulfill My great command and commission. Stop complaining and *go*! Stop whining and *go*! Stop procrastinating and *go*! Stop wasting time and *go*!" He expected

---

[2]   Christopher Benfield. "Reviving the Great Commission" Pulpit Pages - New Testament Sermons (Cross ebook, October 10, 2014)

the disciples to spread the Word of God to the ends of the earth and preach it, in season and out of season, to a dying world. This is not an option.

If you are saved, then that makes you part of the church. This command is also a command Jesus intends for you to obey. We are to go and fulfill this awesome commission. This cannot be accomplished by sitting in a pew within our comfort zone. It cannot be met while we argue over the color of the carpet. It cannot be adequately carried out if we never leave the board room, the finance room, the fellowship hall, or the narthex.

We must be obedient and go outside of the church, outside of the physical building, and retrieve God's lost luggage by telling the world about the good news of Christ (John 3:16). There is still work to do in our communities. There is still work to do in our homes. There is still work to do in the workplace. We have work to do. The work is to spread the gospel message to a world that really needs Jesus.

WE HAVE THE COMFORT OF CHRIST

That's right! Jesus has promised us that while we seek out those who are lost, we need not be afraid, because the One who has "all power" and authority will be with us every step of the way.

I remember once I was walking from the home of my stepmother, Ruby Dale Fletcher, to my birth mother Annie Mae's home. Even though her name was Ruby Dale, I always affectionately called my stepmother "Ru Dear." When I was a youngster, Ru Dear lived in a neighborhood called Jackson Hill, on Adams Street. Annie Mae lived on Spring Street. These streets are located within the same city limits but in different parts of town. What separates the two neighborhoods is very long and steep valley on a street named Wood Street.

One day, when I was old enough to walk from Adams Street to Spring Street alone, there was a group of youngsters about my age who took issue that I was walking by their house. They threw rocks at me, hurled derogatory comments at me, and even chased after me. Though their chase lasted for only a block or so, I kept running because I did not know if they would regain their composure and restart the chase.

Weeks later, I was walking home from Ru Dear's house by that same house. The same group of kids was outside playing. I thought about walking across the street, but it was too late—I was already in front of their house. Hoping they would not notice me, I walked as quickly as I could.

Then they spotted me. My heart raced, but I did not run. I embraced what I surely thought would be a fight and chase. They stopped playing and looked at me. They picked up rocks. They began to walk toward me. I walked even faster.

I was ready to run again, but something strange was going on. This time they did not chase after me, they did not throw rocks at me, nor did they hurl any derogatory comments my way. They only stared at me, with rocks still in their hands. As I continued past their house, they did not throw the rocks. They only stared.

Then they looked behind me. They looked at me again, and then once more behind me with several quick glances. Wanting to figure out what was going on, I turned to look. To my surprise, my older sister Merlean was walking directly behind me. No wonder they dared not tease, throw rocks or chase after me. My big sister, my protector, and my comforter *were with me!*

And this is the comfort that we have in Jesus. When we must walk through the valley of life and disappointment, He is with us always!

For Further Discussion and Reflection:

1. In your opinion, what ways might the twenty-first-century local church fall short of her mission?
2. How did you feel when you lost something of tremendous value to you?
3. How did you feel when what you lost was recovered?
4. In your opinion, what does it mean to the Christian that Jesus has "all power"?
5. In your opinion, what can the individual Christian do to help the local church carry out the mission of the church?

Chapter 3

A Prescription for a Happy Life

*Day 2 continued, Friday, August 28, 2009: Travel
from the States to Galilee and Tiberias*

Mount of Beatitudes Retreat Center and the Church of the Beatitudes

While in Galilee, we had the pleasure and privilege of resorting at the Mount of Beatitudes Retreat Center. The place was extremely accommodating. We had plenty of space to move around, whether within the retreat center buildings or outside on the grounds.

Retreat center where we stayed while in Galilee

This beautiful retreat center sits directly next to the Church of the Beatitudes on top of the mountain where Jesus preached the Sermon on the Mount. It is one of the most attractive works my eyes have ever seen. Each of the eight sides of the church is dedicated to one of the first eight Beatitudes, written in Latin inside the church. The ninth Beatitude (blessed are those who suffer persecution for the sake of Jesus) is symbolized by the dome itself, reaching toward heaven.

Each morning, I would rise early, before our group breakfast, for private meditation on the grounds. One morning during my personal devotional, I was again struggling with this whole idea of lost luggage in a foreign country. I had no clothes to change into. It was a very uncomfortable situation, to say the least, without adequate assistance from the Israeli airline.

Intently, I talked to God about staying at a place called Beatitudes when I was experiencing a "bad attitude" because of my lost luggage. God does have a sense of humor. My good attitude meter was extremely low, and God had placed me in a position on a hill called Mount of Beatitudes to deal with my bad attitude.

James reminds us to "count it all joy when ye fall into divers temptations; Knowing this, that the trying of your faith worketh patience. But let patience have her perfect work, that ye may be perfect and entire, wanting nothing" (James 1:2–4). The only thing I was counting was how long I had been without my luggage. Not a good attitude.

Church of the Beatitudes in Galilee

SCRIPTURE REFLECTION: MATTHEW 5:1–12 KJV

And seeing the multitudes, he went up into a mountain: and when he was set, his disciples came unto him: And he opened his mouth, and taught them, saying, Blessed are the poor in spirit: for theirs is the kingdom of heaven. Blessed are they that mourn: for they shall be comforted. Blessed are the meek: for they shall inherit the earth. Blessed are they which do hunger and thirst after righteousness: for they shall be filled. Blessed are the merciful: for they shall obtain mercy. Blessed are the pure in heart: for they shall see God. Blessed are the peacemakers: for they shall be called the children of God. Blessed are they which are persecuted for righteousness' sake: for theirs is the kingdom of heaven. Blessed are ye, when men shall revile you, and persecute you, and shall say all manner of evil against you falsely, for my sake. Rejoice, and be exceeding glad: for great is your reward in heaven: for so persecuted they the prophets which were before you.

THE DEVOTIONAL

Every year around November or December, someone in our home seems to find their way to visit our family doctor for medication due to a cold or the flu. This past year it was my turn. My entire body ached and pained. I could barely walk. When I finally made it to my doctor's office, he checked and poked on me and finally wrote out a prescription. I smiled and made a beeline to the pharmacy.

You see, I understand something about prescriptions. A prescription is a set of instructions written by a medical doctor that authorizes a patient to be provided a medicine or some kind of treatment. My doctor gave authorization for the pharmacist to provide me a medication designed to help cure my ailment.

The Beatitudes passage of Scripture is a prescription, a set of instructions written by the Doctor of all doctors. The instructions are such that if followed, true happiness will result.

Doctor Jesus began His Sermon on the Mount with the word *blessed*. *Blessed* means "happy" or "fortunate." Blessed qualities or characteristics are primarily internal, not external. Most often people strive to live happy lives, thinking that true happiness is dependent upon the happenings in a person's life. However, true or lasting happiness can only come from God. True happiness does not depend on what's happening in the life of a Christian. It is an inner quality of peace and contentment that is of the heart. It is spiritual. It is not based on a physical set of circumstances, but upon a spiritual relationship with the Lord.

Jesus is saying to us today that life in the kingdom with him is a life of profound joy, a joy that no person and no circumstance can take away. And this blessedness is not reserved for the distant future. It is for right now! Happiness on this level is the mark of those who have surrendered to the King of Kings and Lord of Lords. How fitting that I struggled with my happiness on the very mountain where Jesus challenged us to be happy, no matter how severe our circumstances.

Notice that Jesus chose a mountainside for the purpose of teaching his disciples. This particular mountain was a good sounding board of the sea and made for excellent acoustics for large numbers of people. On some mornings while in Galilee, I went to the Jesus Cave, the traditional cave where Jesus would often retreat to pray. It was located near the Mount of Beatitudes. Sitting there, I could hear voices from several hundred yards away. The acoustics were amazingly clear.

THE BEATITUDES

1. Blessed are the *poor in spirit*—Those who realize they are completely poor or spiritually bankrupt before God. They have come to grips that they are unable to give anything of substance to God on their own and therefore depend totally upon God.

2. Blessed are *those who mourn*—Those who are happy in spirit because they realize that Jesus came to bind up the brokenhearted (Isa. 61:1).

3. Blessed are *the meek*—Those who are happy because they understand their position before God. They are neither too high-minded nor too low-minded, but right-minded about who they are in Jesus Christ (Rom. 12:3).

4. Blessed are those *who hunger and thirst*—Those who are happy in spirit because they have hunger pains and are thirsty for the goodness and righteousness of God.

5. Blessed are the *merciful*—Those who understand that spiritual happiness exists when mercy is extended to others because it was first extended to us by God. Mercy is being kind, generous, forgiving, and compassionate. It is treating others like we want others to treat us.

6. Blessed are the *pure in heart*—Those who are honest, sincere, filled with integrity, and fully committed to the Lord.

7. Blessed are the *peacemakers*—Those who are proactive in making peace that results in reconciliation. Authentic peacemakers seek peace because they are reflecting their Father's character.

8. Blessed are those who have been *persecuted for righteousness' sake*—Those who are persecuted not for doing something wrong, but rather for doing something right. The persecuted are often mistreated because they want what is right. They are sometimes ostracized because they do not choose sides of issues but rather choose the side of what is right.

9. Blessed are those who are *reproached, persecuted and evil spoken of* because of their relationship with Jesus—When we stand on the side of Jesus, we are shining lights of His glory. Light exposes darkness. People of darkness hate the light because the light exposes their sin. The blessing is that those who suffer for the sake of Christ can rest assured that Jesus will walk through the furnace of reproach, persecution, and insults beside His faithful children (Isa. 43:2).

This is the prescription for a happy life. It is paradoxical but immensely profound. I was physically in the Holy Land, standing on holy ground where Jesus, my Savior, preached this dynamic message on the prescription for a happy life, and paradoxically I was refusing to swallow the medication.

For Further Discussion and Reflection:

1. What could the Sermon on the Mount really mean to the twenty-first-century believer?
2. What meaning does the word *blessed* have in your life?
3. What does it mean to be "poor in spirit"?
4. What does it mean to be a part of the kingdom of hearts?
5. What is it about the kingdom that makes it "hard"?
6. How should a person in a right relationship with God conduct herself or himself?
7. Have you ever been persecuted for doing what was right? Did it surprise you how you were treated?

Chapter 4

MOVING TO THE NEXT LEVEL

Day 3, Saturday, August 29, 2009: Arbel and Capernaum

EXCURSION BACKGROUND

On day 3 of the pilgrimage, we went to Capernaum and the Arbel Cliff. The Arbel Cliff is a large mountain. On a clear day you can enjoy a fantastic panoramic view of the northern shores of the Sea of Galilee, the scene of much of Jesus's Galilean ministry.

I vividly remember how excited I was on this morning. In spite of lost luggage and all, I had had a relatively good night of rest and was eager to start the journey of a lifetime. The good rest was because of exhaustion from dealing with airline officials and because of the thoughtful prayers and personal concern of my fellow pilgrims. One pilgrim in particular, Curnell Graham, was very insightful and skillful in helping me gain proper perspective in preparation for the day's activities of walking in the footsteps of Jesus. Even though I had a better perspective, I was still a bit anxious about not knowing when or if my luggage was going to be returned.

Major, standing atop Arbel Cliff with the Sea of Galilee behind

So this day was going to be a splendid day for me and our pilgrimage team. I was amazed at the size of the mountain we were about to walk up. To get to the top, one must follow a trail that involves walking up a gradual slope on the back side of the cliff. It takes about twenty minutes of continuous walking.

I grew weary within the first few minutes of walking, since I was completely out of shape. But because of my personal pride in being a former athlete, I did not allow myself to fall too far behind the group. Amusingly, I also remember trying to disguise my huffing and puffing along the way. I sang to myself between pants, "Feet, don't fail me now!" Glory be to God, they did not fail—at least, not then. I made it to the top triumphantly.

Oh, the feelings of excitement and anticipation of what it would be like to walk in the steps of Jesus in Capernaum still yield many emotions. It was very difficult for me to listen attentively to Claudia, the Galilean guide, because I was preoccupied with taking pictures of the ruins of a local synagogue, where Jesus would have taught. Peter's home, where Jesus healed Peter's mother-in-law, is nearby.

Pilgrims (Cynthia Davis, J. W. Park, Lina Duling-Moore, and Mary Nesmith) viewing the ruins

Capernaum played a central role in Jesus's Galilean ministry (Matt. 4:13; Mark 1:21; Luke 7:1, 10:15; John 6:59). In all likelihood, Capernaum was founded sometime after the Jews returned from captivity. By the New Testament era, Capernaum was large enough that it always was called a city (Matt. 9:1; Mark 1:33). It had its own synagogue, in which Jesus frequently taught (Mark 1:21; Luke

4:31–38; John 6:59). Apparently the synagogue was built by the Roman soldiers garrisoned in Capernaum (Matt. 8:8; Luke 7:1–10).[3] After being rejected in His hometown, Nazareth, Jesus made Capernaum the center of His ministry in Galilee. He performed many miracles here, including the healings of the centurion's paralyzed servant (Matt. 8:5–13), a paralytic carried by four friends (Mark 2:1–12), Peter's mother-in-law (Matt. 8:14–15; Mark 1:29–31), and the nobleman's son (John 4:46–54).

As Jesus walked by the Sea of Galilee near Capernaum, He called the fishermen Simon, Andrew, James, and John to be his disciples (Mark 1:16–21, 29). It was also in "His own city" that Jesus called the tax collector Matthew (Matt. 9:1, 9; Mark 2:13–14). Immediately following the feeding of the five thousand, Jesus delivered His discourse on the Bread of Life near Capernaum (John 6:32).

Although Jesus focused His ministry in Capernaum, the people of that city did not follow him. Jesus pronounced a curse on the town for its unbelief (Matt. 11:23–24), predicting its ruin (Luke 10:15).

SCRIPTURE REFLECTION: MATTHEW 4:12–22 KJV

Now when Jesus had heard that John was cast into prison, he departed into Galilee; And leaving Nazareth, he came and dwelt in Capernaum, which is upon the sea coast, in the borders of Zabulon and Nephthalim: That it might be fulfilled which was spoken by Esaias the prophet, saying, The land of Zabulon, and the land of Nephthalim, by the way of the sea, beyond Jordan, Galilee of the Gentiles; The people which sat in darkness saw great light; and to them which sat in the region and shadow of

3 Max Miller. *A Pilgrimage to the Holy Land,* Holy Land Pastoral Renewal Program (CF Foundation, 2009), 16.

death light is sprung up. From that time Jesus began to preach, and to say, Repent: for the kingdom of heaven is at hand. And Jesus, walking by the sea of Galilee, saw two brethren, Simon called Peter, and Andrew his brother, casting a net into the sea: for they were fishers. And he saith unto them, Follow me, and I will make you fishers of men. And they straightway left their nets, and followed him. And going on from thence, he saw other two brethren, James the son of Zebedee, and John his brother, in a ship with Zebedee their father, mending their nets; and he called them. And they immediately left the ship and their father, and followed him.

THE DEVOTIONAL

When Jesus learned of John the Baptist's imprisonment, He went from Nazareth and settled in Capernaum. The reason he left Nazareth was because the populace rejected His message and could not get beyond knowing Him as the carpenter's son (Luke 4:16–30). This particular region had been settled by the tribes of Zebulun and Naphtali after the conquest of Joshua's time. Isaiah had prophesied that light would come to this region (Isa. 9:1–2), and Matthew saw Jesus's movement as the fulfillment of this prophecy. One of the Messiah's works was to bring light into darkness, for He would be a light to both Jews and Gentiles (John 1:9, 12:46).

Jesus called men from their ordinary pursuits of life to follow him. This was not the first time these men had met Jesus, for the book of John records Jesus's first meeting with some of the disciples (John 1:35–42). Jesus took these men from fishing for fish and gradually converted them to become fishers of men. The message of the coming kingdom needed to be proclaimed widely so that many could hear and could become, by repentance, subjects of the Lord.

The calling carried with it a cost, for it involved leaving not only one's profession but also one's family responsibilities. Matthew noted that James and John left their fishing and also their father to follow Jesus. It should also be stated the disciples did not leave their families or their professions without first making proper provisions for them. Even though they were walking and working with the Savior, their families still needed daily care. Jesus would not have called these men away from their familial responsibilities without allowing for proper care to be put in place (1 Tim. 5:8).

WHEN MOVING TO THE NEXT LEVEL

The text lets us know that Jesus moved from Nazareth, his hometown, to Capernaum, about twenty miles farther north. Why did Jesus move His ministry?

1. To get away from intense opposition in Nazareth.
2. To have an impact on the greatest number of people. Capernaum was a busy city, and Jesus's message could reach more people and spread more quickly.
3. To utilize extra resources and support for his ministry.
4. To fulfill the prophecy of Isaiah 9:1–2, which states that the Messiah would be a light to the land of Zebulun and Naphtali, the region of Galilee where Capernaum is located.

The people of Nazareth could not get past the fact that He was the same Jesus who probably grew up playing with their children. He had run up and down the neighborhood streets. He was the carpenter's son, Mary's little boy, James, Joses, Simon, and Judas's big brother, not to mention his little sisters (Matt. 13:55–57).

Likewise, the children of God must recognize God's timing in moving on to the next level of life and ministry. Recognition of God's timing can be very difficult because many times we are simply caught up in the "now" of life. One way to achieve this recognition is to remain reflective on a regular basis through prayer and devotion.

What are some of the indications that it is time to move on? There will sometimes be intense opposition in your current context of life and ministry. Opposition should not be the only indicator you consider when making a decision to move to the next level. Some opposition can be beneficial because it causes us to pray more often, keeping one's prayer life fresh and operative. Jesus moved to the next level of ministry when opposition reached the level at which His ministry would be negatively impacted. When opposition reaches the level of unbelief, it may be time to move to the next level.

ON BEING LIGHT REFLECTORS IN DARK PLACES

In Matthew 4:16, Matthew quoted Isaiah (see Isa. 9:1–2). The prophet wrote about people who walked in darkness. By the time Matthew quoted the passage, the situation was so dangerous and awful that the people were "sitting" in darkness. But God sent Jesus to bring light to them. He made His headquarters in Capernaum, in "Galilee of the Gentiles," which is another reference to the universal outreach of the gospel's message.[4]

So how did Jesus bring this light to Galilee? According to Matthew 4:23, He brought the light through His teaching, preaching, and healing. This emphasis is found often in the gospel of Matthew (see 9:35, 11:4–5; 12:15; 14:34–36; 15:30; 19:2). In John 1:4–5, Jesus reminds us that He is the source, the creator of the light that gives life to men. In His light, we see ourselves as we are: sinners in need of a Savior. When we follow Jesus, the true light, we can avoid walking blindly and falling into sin. He lights the path ahead of us so we can see how to live. With Jesus guiding our lives, we will never stumble in darkness.

---

[4]   Warren W. Wiersbe, *The Bible Exposition Commentary*, New Testament Vol.1 (Colorado Springs: Cook, 2001), 19.

It must be understood that we are not the source of God's light. We merely reflect that light. Jesus Christ is the true Light, and He helps us see our way to God. Christ has chosen to reflect His light through his followers to an unbelieving world. We are never to present ourselves as the light to others. We should always point them to the true Light, Jesus Christ.

When Jesus called His disciples, part of His discipleship strategy was to train them to continue His ministry. His disciples were to reflect light into dark places, that men, women, and children might no longer walk or sit in darkness.

We, as His modern-day disciples, are called to make dark places our Capernaum headquarters, reaching out and reflecting the light of Jesus. We are to reflect in such a way that people will come running and say, "What must I do to be saved?"(Acts 16:30). We must allow His light to shine reflectively through us while we teach His ways, preach His Word, and heal His people by lending helping hands.

REPENT TO ENJOY FULL FELLOWSHIP WITH GOD

When John the Baptist was imprisoned, Jesus began to preach. His words had a familiar ring: "Repent, for the kingdom of heaven, is at hand" (Matthew 3:2). Jesus now proclaimed the twofold message of John. The work of God was rapidly moving toward the establishment of the glorious kingdom of God on earth. If one wanted to be a part of this kingdom, one must repent.

Repentance is mandatory if true fellowship with God is to be enjoyed. This seems to be a missing ingredient in the twenty-first-century church. Too many individuals appear to think that just "joining" a church is true repentance. Far too many church people believe that giving the preacher your hand, when you go down to the front of the church after an invitation is given, means that repentance has taken place. In many cases, it has not.

What is repentance? The *Nelson's New Illustrated Bible Dictionary* says that repentance is a turning away from sin, disobedience, or rebellion and a turning back to God (Matt. 9:13; Luke 5:32). In a more general sense, repentance means a change of mind (Gen. 6:6–7) or a feeling of remorse or regret for past conduct (Matt. 27:3). True repentance is a "godly sorrow" for sin, an act of turning around and going in the opposite direction. This type of repentance leads to a fundamental change in a person's relationship to God.[5] Just because a person physically responds to an invitation to come to the front of the church or fills out a card and places it in an offering basket does not mean that a "godly sorrow" for one's sin has occurred.

Repentance demonstrates the reality of faith. Confession of sins and a changed life are inseparable. Faith without works is dead (James 2:14–26). In Luke 3:7–8, Jesus spoke some harsh words to the respectable religious leaders who lacked the desire for real change. They wanted to be known as religious authorities, but they didn't intend to change their hearts and minds. Thus, their lives were unproductive. Repentance must be tied to action, or it isn't real. Additionally, this action must be consistent over a period of time.

Repentance does not mean that one is perfect and without sin, for no one is without sin, except Jesus (Rom. 3:23). However, true repentance will be evident by how we live before God, who knows all. Following Jesus means more than saying the right words. It means acting in the right way by doing what He says to do.

THINK LIKE FISHERMEN

Why did Jesus choose fishermen as his first disciples? The term "fishers of men" was not new. For centuries, Greek and Roman philosophers had used it to describe the work of the man who seeks to "catch" others by teaching and persuasion. "Fishing for men" is

---

[5]   R. F. Youngblood. *Nelson's New Illustrated Bible Dictionary.* (Thomas Nelson, Nashville, 1995),1077.

but one of the many pictures of evangelism in the Bible, and we must not limit ourselves to it. Jesus also talked about the shepherd seeking the lost sheep (Luke 15:1–7), and the workers in the harvest field (John 4:34–38). Since these four men were involved in the fishing business, it was logical for Jesus to use that approach.

There were many links between their daily work and the new task Jesus brought them. A skilled fisherman had to know that for the different types of fish found in the Sea of Galilee, different nets needed to be used. A skilled fisherman would also have understood that lack of teamwork could lose him his catch, and lack of patience could leave his nets empty. The choice of the right fishing grounds and sensitivity to nuances of wind, depth, and temperature had to be second nature to him in order to bring in the catch.

Likewise, as fishers of men for God, we must be aware of the various methods or nets to be used to reel in the lost sinners of the world. We must understand the importance of teamwork, the dynamics of working together to position the church to catch those who are swimming aimlessly and without awareness of their need for God. We must also possess a unique sensitivity to the nuances of time, place, and mood when witnessing to people about the goodness of God's salvation.

Kim Hall taking a picture of Major standing on the shores of the Sea of Galilee, in front of Peter's home

Another reason Jesus called fishermen to His side was that they were busy people. Usually, professional fishermen did not sit around doing nothing. They were sorting their catch, cleaning their catch, preparing to catch, or mending their equipment. The Lord is looking for busy people who are not afraid to work.

Fishermen have to be courageous and patient people. It certainly takes patience and courage to win others to Christ. Fishermen must have skill; they must learn from others where to find the fish and how to catch them. Soul-winning demands skill too. But most of all, fishing requires faith. Fishermen cannot see the fish and are not sure their nets will enclose them. Soul-winning requires faith and alertness too. Or we will fail.

Finally, fishermen must work together to bring in a good catch of fish. In Luke 10:1–3, Jesus sent out thirty-five teams of two to reach the multitudes. Jesus did this to emphasize the need for teamwork in ministry. The pastors, deacons, and other ministries within the church must cooperate to bring about a sense of teamwork. Isaiah told the people of God, "Come now, and let us reason together, saith the LORD" (Isa. 1:18).

Jesus also knew that witnessing and evangelizing were best done when you had someone helping you. There is no need for us to try and outdo one another. There is enough work for everybody!

For Further Discussion and Reflection:

1. What does "moving to the next level of ministry" mean to you?
2. What are some necessary things to consider when Christians accept the call of Christ to go to the next level of ministry?
3. How does one know when it is time to move to the next level of ministry?
4. From your perspective, how can today's Disciples of Christ bring light in dark places?
5. In your opinion, what does repentance have to do with being fishers for Christ?
6. Different types of fishing nets were used during Jesus's day to catch fish. What kinds of "fishing nets" do you think are available to Christians to "fish" for unbelievers today?
7. What are some ways in which today's fishers for Christ can collaborate to reach out to their immediate community?

Chapter 5

HAVING BREAKFAST WITH JESUS

Day 4, Sunday, August 30, 2009: Mount of Beatitudes, Tabgha, Primacy of Peter

EXCURSION BACKGROUND

On day 4, our journey was filled with spiritual activities. We spent our day worshipping on the Mount of Beatitudes, visiting Tabgha, the traditional site of the miracle of the loaves and fishes, and the Primacy of Peter.

The locations of some of the events recorded in the gospel narratives are unknown. While we cannot know exactly where some critical moments in Jesus's ministry occurred, pilgrims through the ages have found their way to certain "traditional" places. These places may not be the exact spot, but they seem to fit the narrative.

CHURCH OF THE PRIMACY OF PETER

This church is immediately east of Tabgha along the seashore (about two hundred yards away) but must be reached by the main road. It was built over another rock known as the Mensa Domini, the Lord's Table, that marks the spot where, according to tradition,

Jesus had breakfast with the disciples after their miraculous catch of fish. The church grounds are shaded by trees and provide access to the sea.

Major, sitting on the Mensa Domini, the Lord's Table

SCRIPTURE REFLECTION: JOHN 21:1–19 KJV

> After these things Jesus shewed himself again to the disciples at the sea of Tiberias; and on this wise shewed he himself. There were together Simon Peter, and Thomas called Didymus, and Nathanael of Cana in Galilee, and the sons of Zebedee, and two other of his disciples. Simon Peter saith unto them, I go a fishing. They say unto him, We also go with thee. They went forth, and entered into a ship immediately; and that night they caught nothing. But when the morning was now come, Jesus stood

on the shore: but the disciples knew not that it was Jesus. Then Jesus saith unto them, Children, have ye any meat? They answered him, No. And he said unto them, Cast the net on the right side of the ship, and ye shall find. They cast therefore, and now they were not able to draw it for the multitude of fishes. Therefore that disciple whom Jesus loved saith unto Peter, It is the Lord. Now when Simon Peter heard that it was the Lord, he girt his fisher's coat unto him, (for he was naked,) and did cast himself into the sea. And the other disciples came in a little ship; (for they were not far from land, but as it were two hundred cubits,) dragging the net with fishes. As soon then as they were come to land, they saw a fire of coals there, and fish laid thereon, and bread. Jesus saith unto them, Bring of the fish which ye have now caught. Simon Peter went up, and drew the net to land full of great fishes, an hundred and fifty and three: and for all there were so many, yet was not the net broken. Jesus saith unto them, Come and dine. And none of the disciples durst ask him, Who art thou? knowing that it was the Lord. Jesus then cometh, and taketh bread, and giveth them, and fish likewise. This is now the third time that Jesus shewed himself to his disciples, after that he was risen from the dead. So when they had dined, Jesus saith to Simon Peter, Simon, son of Jonas, lovest thou me more than these? He saith unto him, Yea, Lord; thou knowest that I love thee. He saith unto him, Feed my lambs. He saith to him again the second time, Simon, son of Jonas, lovest thou me? He saith unto him, Yea, Lord; thou knowest that I love thee. He saith unto him, Feed my sheep. He saith unto him the third time, Simon, son of Jonas, lovest thou

me? Peter was grieved because he said unto him the
third time, Lovest thou me? And he said unto him,
Lord, thou knowest all things; thou knowest that I
love thee. Jesus saith unto him, Feed my sheep.

THE DEVOTIONAL

I once heard the story of a man who had not been to church
for a long time. This man used to be a very committed and faithful
member. For some reason he stopped going, and the pastor became
so concerned that he visited the man's home to find out why.

The man invited the pastor into the living room, where the
fireplace was burning. After small talk, the pastor got around to
asking why it was that the man had stopped going to church. The
man replied that he felt he could worship just as faithfully at home
He believed he could get along just fine without the fellowship of
other Christians.

After a few minutes of silence, the pastor got up, took the tongs,
and removed one red-hot log from the pile of logs. He laid the red-
hot log off to the side by itself. Soon they both noticed that the
red-hot lone log lost its glow. The pastor got up and said good-bye.

The very next Sunday, the man was at church.

The point is, just as the lone log needed the other red-hot logs to
maintain its heat and glow, we need the fellowship of Jesus Christ.

In this passage of Scripture, we are invited to look in on a scene
in which the disciples had lost their red-hot glow and were in need of
restoration and fellowship with the Master. A few days earlier, they
all had deserted Jesus immediately following his arrest in the garden
of Gethsemane. Peter denied even knowing Jesus when confronted.

As we look into how the Lord ministered to Peter and the
disciples, pay attention to how Jesus restores them to Himself. If
Jesus can do it for Peter and the other disciples, surely He can do it
for me and you.

JESUS WILL FIND YOU

As a little boy growing up in Muskegon, Michigan, I used to play a neighborhood outdoors game called hide-and-seek. The goal of the game was to hide so that the person seeking you could not find you. We hid in unimaginable places in order not to be found. We would hide in bushes, in empty garbage cans, and beneath abandoned cars. We would sometimes climb trees to blend in with the leaves. But a good seeker would always find us, no matter where we tried to hide.

I have found that Jesus is a very good seeker. He has an all-seeing eye. Proverbs 15:3 reminds us that His eyes are in every place. No matter where we try to run or hide, He already knows where we are.

In this passage, Jesus seeks and shows himself to some of His disciples. "This is now the third time that Jesus shewed himself to his disciples, after that he was risen from the dead" (v.14). Jesus restores the disciples to himself.

Notice three things about the disciples' process of restoration. The first thing the Disciples do is admit failure (v. 5). In coming home to God, there must be an acknowledgment of sin or confession for the wrongful act or acts. The Prodigal Son realized that confession of sin and wrongful acts was necessary (Luke 15:18).

The second thing the disciples do is decide to obey Jesus Christ. They cast their net on the "right" side of the boat, when previously they had been casting on the "wrong" side of the boat.

The third thing is that Peter develops a greater sense of wanting to be close to the Lord (v. 7). Peter stops fishing and goes in the direction of Jesus. He wants to be closer to His Lord. This was also true of the Prodigal Son (Luke 15:20a).

Perhaps you or someone you know is one of those who have walked or wandered away from the Lord. Maybe you, like many others, have drifted into a far country of rebellion or disobedience. If so, you need to know that you still have a friend in Jesus. Jesus still knows your name. He still remembers who you are. He will never leave you or forsake you. He will always love you!

Today, Jesus is standing with open hands of forgiveness and grace toward you and me. He wants us to come to the same place Peter did. He wants us to make our way to the Lord to receive the blessings He has in store for those who seek restoration, discipleship, and fellowship with Him.

JESUS WILL FEED YOU

During my middle school and high school years, there was a group of us guys who used to hang out at our best buddy Rafi's home. When we visited on Saturday mornings, it was extra special, because his mother (I called her Momma Townsend) would have baked delicious homemade biscuits for breakfast. Somehow or another, Mrs. Townsend knew that we were coming over, and the biscuits were waiting for us. No matter what time of the day we showed up, there was always something to eat—including homemade biscuits.

In the same way, no matter what time of day it is in your life, Jesus will always have a meal prepared for you. No matter what the hour, Jesus has a plate of grace for you to eat and a glass of mercy for you to drink. As an appetizer, He serves a helping of peace. And of course, there is dessert. For dessert He serves up joy!

When Peter and the other disciples finally made it to the shore, they discovered that Jesus was preparing a meal for them to eat. They walked into an open breakfast invitation with the Master Cook. It was time to eat! Jesus had prepared a breakfast that provided them everything they needed. The very things they had lacked while attempting to fish—food and fellowship—Jesus was already preparing to give to them on the shore. All they had to do was come to breakfast with Jesus. They found a Savior who loved them.

Maybe you are one who is currently dealing with feelings of remorse, misery, lack of peace, and lack of joy in your life because of your past. Let me encourage you. We serve a God who is standing by, ready and willing to feed us whatever we need. He has all the things you lacked while you were away from Him.

I am here to tell you that if you return to the Father today, you will find that He has everything you need. He has water for the thirsty, food for the hungry, sight for the blind, strength for the weak, help for the hopeless, victory for the defeated, joy for the sorrowful, and a compass for those who are lost. What a mighty God we serve! He loves you and desires to have close fellowship with you.

Regardless of how far you may have moved away from God, Jesus is standing on the shore of forgiveness and is proclaiming, "Come and dine" (v.12). We have a wonderful friend in Jesus, and He now invites each of us to breakfast. The only question to be answered is, are you coming?

For Further Discussion and Reflection:

1. Why do you think it is important to confess one's sin and failures while seeking forgiveness and restoration?
2. When the Lord found Peter, Peter was fishing and had no clothes on. What were you doing when the Lord found you?
3. What comes to your mind when you think about the title "Having Breakfast with Jesus"?
4. What about the friendship of Jesus do you most enjoy?

Chapter 6

HAVING LUNCH WITH JESUS

Day 4 continued, Sunday, August 30, 2009: Mount
of Beatitudes, Tabgha, Primacy of Peter

*Tabgha, the traditional site where Jesus fed 5000
men with two fish and five loaves of bread*

EXCURSION BACKGROUND

On this day, we visited Tabgha, the place where, tradition says,
Jesus fed five thousand men (plus women and children) with two
fish and five loaves of bread. It is located at the foot of the Mount of
Beatitudes, on the northwest shores of the Sea of Galilee. Tabgha,
an Arabic name, is derived from Greek *heptapegon*, which means
"seven springs."

This visit was extremely exhilarating for me because this passage of Scripture is one of my personal favorites to teach and preach. I will always remember this day for another reason. Many in our group decided they would add more fun to the day by putting on their swimming gear and getting wet in the spring water at Tabgha. I wanted to join the team, but my swimming trunks were in my lost luggage.

There is a church in Tabgha that stands on the spot where the feeding of the five thousand took place. The Benedictines erected the current church building in 1981. The Church of the Multiplication of the Loaves and Fish, shortened to the Church of the Multiplication, is a Roman Catholic church. The modern church rests on the site of two earlier churches. An opening in the floor to the left of the altar allows one to view the foundation walls of the original fourth-century church.

As you enter the church and walk toward what is called the apse or interior ceiling arch, you encounter a raised platform at the opposite end. At its center is an untrimmed stone marking the traditional site of the miracle, where Jesus would have laid the bread.

SCRIPTURE REFLECTION: MATTHEW 14:13–23 KJV

When Jesus heard of it, he departed thence by ship into a desert place apart: and when the people had heard thereof, they followed him on foot out of the cities. And Jesus went forth, and saw a great multitude, and was moved with compassion toward them, and he healed their sick. And when it was evening, his disciples came to him, saying, This is a desert place, and the time is now past; send the multitude away, that they may go into the villages, and buy themselves victuals. But Jesus said unto them, They need not depart; give ye them to eat.

And they say unto him, We have here but five loaves, and two fishes. He said, Bring them hither to me. And he commanded the multitude to sit down on the grass, and took the five loaves, and the two fishes, and looking up to heaven, he blessed, and brake, and gave the loaves to his disciples, and the disciples to the multitude. And they did all eat, and were filled: and they took up of the fragments that remained twelve baskets full. And they that had eaten were about five thousand men, beside women and children. And straightway Jesus constrained his disciples to get into a ship, and to go before him unto the other side, while he sent the multitudes away. And when he had sent the multitudes away, he went up into a mountain apart to pray: and when the evening was come, he was there alone.

THE DEVOTIONAL

A few years ago, one of my favorite people in all the world died suddenly: my nephew Ricky. I was devastated upon receiving the phone call. We had grown up as brothers, being the same age. We traveled the country together. We laughed, cried, and argued together.

When he died, for a time I withdrew into seclusion to get myself together. I needed extra time to myself. I went into my prayer closet to receive spiritual healing from the Lord.

In this passage of Scripture, Jesus had a similar experience. After hearing about his cousin John the Baptist being murdered, our Lord and Savior withdrew from the scenes of society and sought seclusion. Jesus needed time to rest His weary soul along with his disciples. He needed time to teach His team of disciples concerning His approaching death and crucifixion.

Jesus got into a boat to relax as He crossed to the northern part of the Sea of Galilee. However, a multitude of people received word that Jesus was coming, and they followed Him on foot. When the Lord saw this, He was moved with compassion and began healing those who came to him with sickness and disease.

Then he invited the multitude of folk to have lunch with him. With two fishes and five loaves of bread, he fed five thousand men, besides women and children. This miracle is recorded by all four gospel writers. This meant that whatever was discussed was very important.

So what is Jesus trying to tell us?

WHY JESUS PERFORMED THE MIRACLE

The first reason this miracle was performed was to illustrate that Jesus Christ, as the Bread of Life, was to be broken on the cross for the sin of humanity. Second, it was performed to show the Jews that One greater than Moses was here. You see, the Jews revered Moses because they believed that it was Moses who had given the Israelites bread in the wilderness. Jesus reminded them that God gave the Hebrews the manna, but Jesus Himself was the true Bread of God (John 6:32–33). The third reason it was performed was to demonstrate the power of Jesus as the Lord of all creation.

JESUS BLESSED THE LUNCH

Notice what Jesus did. "He blessed." When Christ blessed the food, He gave thanks for it. Other accounts of this event in Scripture confirm this fact.

"Blessed" and "gave thanks" are sometimes used interchangeably in Scripture, and we often use the words interchangeably today to describe giving thanks before a meal. For instance, if we ask a person to say the blessing, we mean for him to give thanks for the food.

It is a good habit to thank God for the food. When people do not thank God for their meal, they are being very forgetful or just plain ungrateful. Moreover, we ought to be very alert to thank God for any and everything we have. It is an excellent life habit to exhibit an attitude of being thankful. It is the divine will of God that each of us understands how essential it is to thank God in every situation in which we find ourselves (1 Thess. 5:18).

WHY JESUS BLESSED THE LUNCH

"Looking up to heaven." This means Christ was giving thanks to God for the food. He did this in order to honor God. Giving thanks honors the Lord.

The Jewish Talmud (a commentary on Jewish history) says, "He that enjoys aught without thanksgiving is as though he robbed God." When one fails to give thanks for his food, he brings dishonor to God. Today most people seem more interested in their stomachs being filled than in honoring God. But failure to thank God for today's food may eventually result in no food tomorrow.

WHERE JESUS BLESSED THE LUNCH

"The multitude." Christ gave thanks for the food in public. There was, in fact, a great multitude present with Christ. The Bible says there were about five thousand men, besides women and children. Christ did not hesitate to thank God for the presence of this magnitude of people.

If God blesses you in public, you should acknowledge it in public. Do not be ashamed to tell God thank you for the food He has blessed you to eat. Failure to give thanks in a public eating place says your Christianity is not worth much. The Lord has been too good to us for us to be concerned about what others may think about us if we display public thanks.

Jesus said, "For whosoever shall be ashamed of me and of my words, of him shall the Son of man be ashamed, when he shall come in his own glory, and in his Father's, and of the holy angels" (Luke 9:26 KJV). Thus, we as children of God should be willing and ready to always give God thanks, both privately and publicly!

WHEN JESUS BLESSED THE LUNCH

"Gave to the disciples." Christ gave thanks before the miracle occurred of the multiplying of the food. When He gave thanks, He only had five loaves and two fish in His hand. Even though Jesus did not have very much, He yet thanked God for what He had.

If you will give thanks for what you have, even if it is not much, rather than complain about what you do not have, you will get along a lot better in life. I remember a preacher once said, "The grateful heart will best experience the gracious and generous benevolence of God." A popular song during my high school days reminded us to "be thankful for what you've got, though you may not drive a great big Cadillac." Powerful thoughts indeed!

For Further Discussion and Reflection:

1. Why is it important to God for us to be thankful for what we have?
2. Why is it important to us for us to be thankful for what we have?
3. What does it mean to be thankful in the context of our relationship with Jesus?
4. Have you ever been guilty of exhibiting an ungrateful attitude? How did the Holy Spirit convict you?
5. Have you ever been ashamed or embarrassed to bless your food in public? Why?

Chapter 7

THE TRAGEDY OF REJECTING JESUS

Day 5, Monday, August 31, 2009: Sepphoris and Nazareth

EXCURSION BACKGROUND

"Another day of excitement," I thought as I finished eating my plentiful breakfast at the Mount of Beatitude's convent.

We left early for the towns of Sepphoris and Nazareth. We visited Sepphoris first. Sepphoris is a village and archeological site located just northwest of Nazareth. In late Christian tradition, it was believed to be the birthplace of the Mary, mother of Jesus. The Hebrew form of Sepphoris is "Zippori," which means "bird." It was so named because the city was perched on the top of a mountain like a bird.

We visited the Roman theater that was built toward the end of the first century, after the First Jewish Revolt had led to the destruction of Jerusalem and the fall of Masada (AD 70–73). The layout of the Roman streets and buildings were impressive. Some of the streets have been excavated, and I could see how there would have been shops and other structures along each side of the streets. There were also the ruins of many synagogues.

Sepphoris is thought to be a city where Jesus and his father Joseph worked during the day, building roads and buildings made of stone. Sepphoris is only about four miles from Nazareth, so it was within walking distance. Carpenters in that day, since wood was very scarce, also worked with stones.

What was really exciting for me was that I most likely stood and walked on the very roads that Jesus himself helped to build. Sepphoris is not mentioned in the Bible but was captured by Herod from Antigonus during the winter of 39–38 BC. Once Herod was established on the throne, Sepphoris served as the northern headquarters of his kingdom.

Major standing on the stone streets of Sepphoris,
which Jesus may have helped to lay

When Herod died in 4 BC, his kingdom was divided among three sons, and Galilee fell to Herod Antipas. This was the Herod who was contemporary with Jesus, and he set about immediately rebuilding Sepphoris as his residence and capital.[6]

From Sepphoris to Nazareth was a short distance. Nazareth was a great place to visit. It was where Jesus grew up. It was considered to be a ghetto or of little importance in its day. In fact, it was Nathanael

---

6   Max Miller. *A Pilgrimage to the Holy Land*, Holy Land Pastoral Renewal Program (CF Foundation, 2009), 25.

who said, "Can there any good thing come out of Nazareth? Philip saith unto him, Come and see" (John 1:46).

Because Nazareth in New Testament times was such a modest settlement, it left little in the way of archeological remains. The village was situated on a rocky hillside, there were caves among the rocks, and when the villagers constructed their houses from fieldstone and mud bricks, they sometimes incorporated caves into their houses. A house might be built over or in front of a cave, for example, with the cave serving as a back room or stable. The mud bricks and fieldstone disappeared over time, so archeological excavations reveal little more than rock surfaces and caves.[7]

Over time, Christians identified what they thought were the house of Joseph and the house of Mary. According to tradition, the angel Gabriel appeared to Mary at her house. Thus, the cave that represents her house is also known as the Grotto of the Annunciation. This is the cave where the angel Gabriel announced the incarnation of Jesus Christ to Mary (Luke 1:26–38).

SCRIPTURE REFLECTION: MARK 6:1–6 KJV

And he went out from thence, and came into his own country; and his disciples follow him. And when the sabbath day was come, he began to teach in the synagogue: and many hearing him were astonished, saying, From whence hath this man these things? and what wisdom is this which is given unto him, that even such mighty works are wrought by his hands? Is not this the carpenter, the son of Mary, the brother of James, and Joses, and of Juda, and Simon? and are not his sisters here with us? And they were offended at him. But Jesus said unto them, A prophet is not without

---

7   Max Miller. *A Pilgrimage to the Holy Land*, Holy Land Pastoral Renewal Program (CF Foundation,2009),29.

> *honour, but in his own country, and among his own kin, and in his own house.*
>
> *And he could there do no mighty work, save that he laid his hands upon a few sick folk, and healed them. And he marvelled because of their unbelief. And he went round about the villages, teaching.*

THE DEVOTIONAL

Life brings with it a measure of rejection. Rejection can be very traumatic to one's self-image. Most people I know, including me, do not like being rejected at all. It doesn't feel good. It's not cute. It's a major turn-off.

Rejection is even worse when it is enacted by someone you know. Growing up in Muskegon, I became a pretty good all-around athlete. I participated in organized sports such as boxing, wrestling, basketball, and football. In my ninth-grade year of high school, I tried out for the ninth-grade basketball team and was eventually cut. I could not believe the coach would actually cut me from the team. I was emotionally devastated and socially embarrassed. At that time in my life, I felt a great sense of rejection. It was extremely difficult for me to digest the fact that I had been cut, especially since I had never been cut from any team up to that point.

Later in life, in the mid-1990s, I was living in the Boston, Massachusetts, area and tried out for a semiprofessional football team. I did not make the final cut. Even though I felt a measure of rejection, it was not devastating at all. In fact, after hearing I was cut, I went out to dinner with some of the fellas who had made the team.

What made the difference in my attitude? The difference was twenty years of growing up. I matured over the years, understanding that a measure of rejection comes with the territory in life. We grow to expect some kinds of rejection from the outside world, from those who do not know us. The real issue with rejection is being rejected by those who truly know who we are.

In this passage of Scripture, we see Jesus being rejected by people who should have known His true identity. These were people who knew His family. They knew His parents. They knew the names of His brothers. They knew the address of the family's carpentry business. They were familiar with His message and miracles.

But they did not know Him as the Messiah! They did not know Jesus as the King of Kings and the Lord of Lords. They did not know Jesus.

You have to be careful when you accept the Lord's message and the Lord's miracles, but not the Lord Himself. We accept Jesus by receiving Him (John 1:12). We accept Jesus by believing in Him (John 3:16). We accept Jesus by confessing Him (Rom. 10:9). The Nazarenes did not really know the identity of Jesus and therefore could not receive Jesus.

Like a skilled surgeon, Jesus cut right to the problem and said, "A prophet is not without honour, but in his own country, and among his own kin, and in his own house" (Mark 6:4). What was Jesus really saying when He said this? First, He was saying that a prophet is without honor in his own country because too many people think they know him *too well.*

It's a cliché that familiarity breeds contempt. This may be true for many, but not for Jesus. The Nazarenes thought, because they grew up with Jesus, that they knew him. They could not understand how someone so familiar to them could be so mighty and powerful.

Second, the Nazarenes had a misconception about what it means to be truly *great.* They rejected Jesus because He was a carpenter. He was Mary and Joseph's oldest boy. He was not a college graduate. The people of Nazareth were expecting a king who would show up looking regal and powerful. They were expecting a fleet of limousines. They allowed their misconception of what true greatness is to blind them from seeing the true Messiah in Jesus Christ.

Even today, we are blinded by misconceptions of what true greatness and value are. Greatness and value cannot be measured by how many letters are behind one's name. Greatness and value cannot be measured by how much money one has in one's bank accounts. Nor can greatness and value be measured by the style of clothes one wears.

True greatness and value come from God. As Christians, we are somebody in Christ. We are a chosen generation, a royal priesthood, an holy nation, a peculiar (God's special possession) people. We are people of great value and worth! (1 Pet. 2:9).

Third, Jesus was saying that a hometown prophet is without honor because he is really *unknown* by the people. Jesus wasn't rejected because they knew Him so well, but because they *thought* they knew Him. Actually, they were unaware of His true mission and identity. They came to conclusions about knowing Him based upon external factors, such as knowing His mother, His brothers, His sisters, and His work as a carpenter. However, they did not know Him.

Just because we attend church does not mean we know Jesus. Just because your mother is a good member of the church does not mean you know Jesus. We must really know Him and be known of Him! We do not want to experience what some will hear from the Lord: "I never knew you: depart from me" (Matt. 7:21–23).

Tragically, because the Nazarenes rejected Jesus, He could not do any mighty and miraculous works in His hometown. When Jesus saw the nature of their rejection, He "marveled at their unbelief." In other words, Jesus stood in wonder and amazement. Jesus was amazed that these people had heard the truth, seen the truth, and still rejected the truth. As a result, He left Nazareth and took His blessings and miracles elsewhere.

If we desire Jesus to be active in our midst, we must not reject Him. If we reject Jesus by rejecting His message, might, and ministry, Jesus will do what He did in Nazareth. He will leave and go elsewhere.

There is a word here for the church. Jesus shows up when we meet, "for where two or three are gathered together in my name, there am I in the midst of them" (Matt. 18:20). Jesus desires to teach us the truth of His Word. He wants us to grow in knowledge and wisdom. If we trust Him and receive Him, we will marvel at what He can do!

For Further Discussion and Reflection:

1. Explain a time in your life when what someone said to you stunned or astonished you.
2. Why do you believe Jesus was not well received in His hometown?
3. Have you ever experienced rejection by people who knew you or watched you grow up? Explain.

Chapter 8

WHAT THE STORMS OF
LIFE CAN TEACH US

*Day 6, Tuesday, September 1, 2009: Boat ride on the
Sea of Galilee, Man in the Galilee Museum*

EXCURSION BACKGROUND

On this day, we visited the Nof Ginosar Kibbutz. A kibbutz, Hebrew
for "communal settlement," is a unique rural community. This
community believes and is committed to mutual aid and social
justice. They are dedicated to a socioeconomic system based on the
principle of joint ownership of property, equality, and cooperation
in production, consumption and education. It is the fulfillment of
the idea of "from each according to his ability, to each according to
his needs." It is a home for those who have chosen it.[8] The food we
ate was surprisingly exquisite. The fellowship was amazing.

The Nof Ginosar Kibbutz is the home to the Yigal Allon Museum
of Man in the Galilee, which houses a two-thousand-year-old fishing
boat called the "Jesus Boat." This small fishing vessel, found at
Ginosar in 1986, gives great insight into biblical passages in which

---

[8] "The Kibbutz and Moshav: History and Overview", Jewish Virtual
Library, n.d. Web. Oct. 2014.

the disciples are described fishing or toiling during a storm (Matt. 14:22–33; Mark 6:45–52), or Jesus is described as preaching from a boat to a crowd assembled on the shore (Luke 5:1–3).

The boat is 19.5 feet long and 7.5 feet wide. It is made entirely of wood, the planks being held together by mortise-and-tenon joints. The frames were installed after the hull had been constructed, rather than the more usual practice of building the hull around the frame. It appears that the boat was crewed by five people, using a sail and two pairs of oars.

The Jesus Boat, discovered in 1986 on the shores of the Sea of Galilee

Next, we boarded a tour boat for an extended boat ride on the Sea of Galilee. Once on the boat, all I could think about was how awesome it was to be on the same body of water upon which Jesus actually walked. It was an amazing thought and experience. The other pilgrims on the boat seemed to be actively taking in this experience in their own ways.

*Pilgrims Cynthia Davis and Kim Hall reflecting
upon the calmness of the Sea of Galilee*

On this day, I was in a much better place spiritually. The peace of God was all over me as I sat there watching, listening, meditating, and praying. I was in tune with the Spirit of God like never before in life. I took in every ray of sun. I was attentive to every wave of water that lightly brushed up against the boat. I heard every word preached by a fellow pilgrim, Rev. Curnell Graham, as he described how Jesus came to the rescue of the storm-stranded disciples. I was so attentive to the word pictures he painted, I was literally motionless. What a day!

ABOUT THE SEA OF GALILEE

The Sea of Galilee is an exquisite and tranquil body of water the Israelis call Lake Kinneret. The banks are 695 feet below sea level.

From north to south, the lake measures about thirteen miles, and its width reaches a maximum of eight miles. The total area is sixty-five square miles. On average it is 161 feet deep. The lake serves as Israel's principal reservoir. The National Water Carrier pipeline pumps water directly from the shore near Capernaum to smaller reservoirs across the country. The "red line" is a theoretical water level below which the lake's surface should not drop, but it has done so frequently in recent years. There is concern about the quality of the water and the effect on its fish.[9]

The Hebrew name for the Sea of Galilee is Yam Kinneret. The name Kinneret comes from *ginner*, meaning "harp," because of its shape. The size and shape of the Sea of Galilee are ideal. Wherever you stand, whether from a distant viewpoint or on the very shore, the countryside can be seen rising steeply on the other side.

The Sea of Galilee, the shores of Capernaum

---

[9] Andrew Sanger. Fodor's Exploring Israel, Canada: Fodor's Travel(2006), 196.

The Sea of Galilee holds a central place in the hearts of millions of people around the world. This, more than anywhere else, is the land of Jesus. He lived on the lakeshore, His disciples were its fishermen, and many of His miraculous works were performed by its banks. Jesus even walked on its water. Additionally, the Jordan River, which many of us sing about, flows into one end of the Sea of Galilee and out of the other. I have found, like many other pilgrims before me, that the very spirit of Jesus and His ministry continues to flow around the shores of the Sea of Galilee.

Scripture Reflection: Matthew 14:22–34 KJV

And straightway Jesus constrained his disciples to get into a ship, and to go before him unto the other side, while he sent the multitudes away. And when he had sent the multitudes away, he went up into a mountain apart to pray: and when the evening was come, he was there alone. But the ship was now in the midst of the sea, tossed with waves: for the wind was contrary.

And in the fourth watch of the night Jesus went unto them, walking on the sea. And when the disciples saw him walking on the sea, they were troubled, saying, It is a spirit; and they cried out for fear. But straightway Jesus spake unto them, saying, Be of good cheer; it is I; be not afraid. And Peter answered him and said, Lord, if it be thou, bid me come unto thee on the water. And he said, Come. And when Peter was come down out of the ship, he walked on the water, to go to Jesus. But when he saw the wind boisterous, he was afraid; and beginning to sink, he cried, saying, Lord, save me. And immediately Jesus stretched forth his hand,

and caught him, and said unto him, O thou of little faith, wherefore didst thou doubt? And when they were come into the ship, the wind ceased. Then they that were in the ship came and worshipped him, saying, Of a truth thou art the Son of God. And when they were gone over, they came into the land of Gennesaret.

THE DEVOTIONAL

Jesus had fed more than five thousand guests. The crowd had been dismissed and were on their way home. Jesus instructed the disciples to pack up, get on the boat and head across the Sea of Galilee to Bethsaida. Jesus then took advantage of some quiet time and went up to a nearby hill to pray.

While Jesus was praying, the disciples departed for their destination, Bethsaida. Unfortunately, the disciples had not traveled very far out on the lake when a strong northwest wind blew against them. They toiled all night long. In fact, it was the fourth watch of the evening (3:00 to 6:00 a.m.), and they were still trying to make it to the other side.

The blessing was that Jesus saw them toiling. He knew exactly where they were in the midst of the storm. At the point of their greatest need, Jesus went walking to their rescue.

Major on a boat, meditatively looking over the Sea of Galilee

As we toured the Sea of Galilee, I could not help but think about this passage of Scripture, where we find the disciples of our Lord trapped in the grip of a fierce storm on this very sea. They found themselves in a storm because they had been commanded by the Lord to cross the Sea of Galilee. The men were struggling because they willingly obeyed the Lord. The disciples were stuck and unable to get out.

Many people at some point have been stuck in a storm and unable to get out. Perhaps as you read this book, you or someone you know is in a storm. Even if you have yet to experience a real-life storm, I guarantee that if you keep living, a storm with your name on it will one day touch down in your life.

Storms come in various forms: financial difficulty, emotional despair, unemployment, relationship troubles, and so on. Even though life storms are ultimately unavoidable, the good news is that they do not last for always. Eventually they will give way to calm and sunshine.

Here is another blessing: while the storms of life are never pleasant, they do produce certain benefits that we might not have realized had it not been for the storms. "Now no chastening for the present seemeth to be joyous, but grievous: nevertheless afterward it yieldeth the peaceable fruit of righteousness unto them which are exercised thereby" (Heb. 12:11).

The good news is the Lord has a blessing called peace that will help us endure while we are yet toiling in the storm. Energized by this peaceable fruit of righteousness, we will pass the test of trials and tribulations with flying colors.

As I think back on my frustrations in dealing with the airlines and the loss of my luggage in a foreign place, it was my personal storm. There I was, on that body of water, in a storm of my own. Even so, luggage or no luggage, it was the sufficient grace of God that calmed my soul with the peaceable fruit of righteousness. What a mighty God we serve!

So the next time you find yourself in the midst of a storm, remember "to count it all joy when ye fall into divers temptations; Knowing this, that the trying of your faith worketh patience" (James 1:2–3). You see, the Lord has a purpose in allowing that storm to rage in your life.

Reflecting back, I believe one of the purposes of God in allowing the temporary loss of my luggage was for me to be "stripped" of excess baggage. It was as if God were saying, "Major, you have too much baggage, too many distractions, too much stuff with you. I need to get your undivided attention in order for you to truly walk in my steps."

I believe that until we mature spiritually to a definite level and are willing to allow the Lord's stripping of excess baggage, we will not be able to appreciate the spiritual blessings God desires for us to realize as we encounter inevitable storms in life.

JESUS COMES TO US IN THE STORMS

In verse 25, the disciples discovered Jesus would come to them while they were yet going through the storm. Jesus, after praying, appeared much later in the night but nevertheless in the midst of the storm.

Jesus will do the same thing for you and me. He will show up at the midnight hour. The Bible says Jesus came to them in "the fourth watch." Sometime between 3:00 a.m. and 6:00 a.m., during the darkest hours of the night, Jesus came walking on the water!

You may be walking in darkness right now and wondering where Jesus is. You may be facing some of the darkest days of your life right now. Let me remind you that our God is ever with you, for the writer of Hebrews says, "For he hath said, I will never leave thee, nor forsake thee" (Heb. 13:5) Even in the darkest hours of life, God is still God, and He is still in control of your life. "If I say, Surely the darkness shall cover me; even the night shall be light about me. Yea, the darkness hideth not from thee; but the night shineth as the day: the darkness and the light are both alike to thee" (Ps. 139:11–12). Even the darkest hours cannot hide you from the face of God. He is there, though you cannot see Him.

The disciples were in a fight for their lives. In Mark 6:48, it says that they were "toiling in rowing." Clearly, they were struggling. They believed all hope was gone and they were doomed. It was then that Jesus came walking on the waves.

I thank God Jesus did come walking on the waves for me during the early part of my journey in the Holy Land. He did not come in the way I expected, but He did come to my rescue. He came in the form of my fellow pilgrims. I was overwhelmed with appreciation for the way the group considered my personal circumstances. The team prayed for me. Each of them, in his or her way, freely shared words of encouragement and concern. One of my brother pilgrims even offered to share his clothes with me, though I think they were a size or two too small. It was the thought that counted.

That day, Jesus came to me. That day, Jesus showed up and reminded me that even though I had to go through my personal storms and frustrations, He cared enough to send the very best, to extend His love and concern for me. I learned a valuable lesson that day. I learned that Jesus will often come to us, walking on the water of our troubles—but we must learn to recognize Him when He shows up!

Perhaps there are times when you feel like you have lost the battle or are losing the battle while in the midst of your storm. I think most of us have been there a time or two. However, what we must understand is that the Lord not only comes to us in the storm, but He is also in charge of the storm. He may not keep us from going into the storm, but He will keep us in the midst of the storm. Just when you think you are at your wits' end, Jesus shows up and Jesus shows out.

Do you recall the three Hebrew boys? Do you recall Daniel? Do you recall Noah? God did not prevent any of these from going into the storm, but He saved all of them in the midst of their storms. What God did for them, He will do for you!

JESUS REVEALS HIMSELF TO US IN THE STORMS

When Jesus came walking on the water, the disciples did not recognize Him. They thought He was a ghost. They cried out in fear.

The storms of life will sometimes reveal Jesus in a way that we do not recognize or comprehend. But glory be to God that Jesus revealed Himself by coming with a message of peace ("be of good cheer") and of power ("It is I"). It is comforting to know that when Jesus comes to us, walking on our storms, He comes with the same message of peace and power: "Be of good cheer; it is I; be not afraid" (Matt. 14:27).

For Further Discussion and Reflection:

1. How has Jesus come to you during times of storms in your life?
2. How has Jesus revealed Himself to you during those storms?
3. How is it possible for your faith to increase during times of storms?
4. What difference does it make for you to know that Jesus is in charge of the storms of life?

Chapter 9

JESUS IS THE REAL THING!

Day 7, Wednesday, September 2, 2009: Banias (Caesarea Philippi)

EXCURSION BACKGROUND

On day 7, we journeyed to Banias, or Caesarea Philippi. Banias is located at the foot of Mount Hermon. It is a beautiful park. A spring in a cave feeds a stream with pools and beautiful falls, which in turn feeds into the Jordan River. This park attracts many visitors, in part because of its extensive classical ruins. I immensely enjoyed listening to the roaring of the water as it flowed downstream to its final destination, the Jordan River.

Major standing in front of a stream that feeds into the Jordan River

Banias was once perhaps the most famous pagan shrine in Israel. The park entrance opens into an impressive Greek archeological site, with pools and statues. Previously sacred to the Canaanite god, Baal, the shrine was rededicated to Pan (Paneas in Greek, from which the name Banias is derived) when it became part of the Hellenistic kingdom of Antiochus III of Syria in the third century BC.

According to Max Miller, author of our pilgrimage handbook, the Romans rededicated the site to Pan and Zeus when they took control of Palestine. Herod's son Philip made Banias his capital, renamed it Caesarea Philippi, and turned it into the biggest city in northern Israel.

Caesarea Philippi was an especially pagan city. It was known for its worship of Greek gods and its temples devoted to the ancient god Baal. The tetrarch Philip, referred to in Mark 6:17, changed the city's name so that it would not be confused with the coastal town of

Caesarea (Acts 8:40). The coastal city was the capital of the territory ruled by his brother Herod Antipas.

Caesarea Philippi, where many gods were recognized, was a fitting place for Jesus to ask the disciples, "But whom say ye that I am?" It later passed into Arab hands, and the city died away. It was held by Crusaders from 1129 to 1135. In 1967, Israel took over, and its population was only 200.[10]

Curnell Graham (left) and Major standing in front of shrine ruins in Caesarea Philippi

The gospel of Matthew (16:13–20) relates that, while visiting Caesarea Philippi and walking beside the water, Jesus asked His disciples who they thought He was. Simon Peter for the first time declared Jesus to be the Messiah, whereupon Jesus called him Petrus, saying, "Upon this rock I will build my church."

---

[10] Max Miller. *A Pilgrimage to the Holy Land*, Holy Land Pastoral Renewal Program (CF Foundation, 2009), 32.

Scripture Reflection: Mark 8:27–30 KJV

> And Jesus went out, and his disciples, into the towns of Caesarea Philippi: and by the way he asked his disciples, saying unto them, Whom do men say that I am? And they answered, John the Baptist: but some say, Elias; and others, One of the prophets. And he saith unto them, But whom say ye that I am? And Peter answereth and saith unto him, Thou art the Christ. And he charged them that they should tell no man of him.

The Devotional

There was a Motown hit song released in 1968, written by Nickolas Ashford and Valerie Simpson and performed by Tammi Terrell and Marvin Gaye, called "Ain't Nothing Like the Real Thing." Tammi and Marvin attempted to communicate soulfully that nothing and no one could replace the authentic relationship and love the two of them shared. They had come to the conclusion that nothing, including pictures and letters, could take the place of the authentic person. They wanted to experience face-to-face, person to person, and touch to touch with one another. They wanted the real thing!

Though Caesarea Philippi appeared to be out of the way of Jesus's journey to Jerusalem, it stood as the religious fortress of the pagan world, challenging His Godhead. Furthermore, Christians in Rome, for whom Mark wrote, needed to know that Jesus Christ, the God to whom they had pledged allegiance, had gone before them to deny the deity of Caesar.

So, in the arena of Caesarea Philippi, where gods dueled to the death, Jesus asked His disciples the question, "Who do you say that

I am?" (v. 29). If He is the Christ, who comes, there is no alternative. There is no other god. Jesus is really the real thing.

The interesting thing about this question is the timing of it all. Jesus knew He would be leaving the scene shortly to die for the sins of mankind. He would be leaving the disciples to carry out the Great Commission. Therefore, it was crucially important for the disciples to understand that it was not enough to know what others said about Jesus. The disciples themselves had to know, understand, and accept that Jesus is the Messiah.

WHAT DO MEN SAY ABOUT JESUS, THE REAL THING?

To test the disciples' power of distinction, Jesus gave them a frame of reference for His first question, "Who do men say that I am?" (v. 27). Even while testing His disciples, He was teaching them.

The disciples knew what people were saying about Jesus. They answered, "John the Baptist; but some say, Elijah; and others [say], one of the prophets" (v. 28). They remembered Herod's response when he first heard of Jesus's fame: "And he said, 'John the Baptist is risen from the dead, and therefore these powers are at work in him'" (6:14).

I agree with Ogilvie and McKenna in their commentary on this passage: "The disciples remembered the speculation of those who contend that the fiery Elijah or one of the other prophets has returned in the Person of Jesus (6:15). These are the half-truths of half-blind men. By the very nature of their answer, the disciples position themselves for a spiritual breakthrough. They have come to the point when they have to decide whether Jesus stands apart from other men in *kind* as He has stood above them in *degree*."[11]

---

[11] David. L. McKenna and Lloyd J. Ogilvie. The Preacher's Commentary (Nashville, TN: Thomas Nelson Inc, 1982),169-172.

WHAT DO YOU SAY ABOUT JESUS, THE REAL THING?

Against the background of men's opinions, Jesus put the critical question to the disciples: "But who do you say that I am?" (v. 29).

On behalf of all the disciples, Peter answered, "You are the Christ" (v. 29).

It is a wonder that the heavens did not open to let all the earth hear the angels singing, "Holy, Holy, Holy, Lord God Almighty." I believe the only reason the heavens kept silent was because the earthly mission of Jesus was not yet finished and the disciples' learning was not yet complete. Peter's confession, "You are the Christ," is proof that the disciples clearly saw who Jesus was. But they did not yet see clearly enough to understand how He would fulfill His mission as the Christ. Wisely, Jesus charged them to hold the truth in confidence until they could handle its full implications.[12]

Today, Jesus continues to ask the same question: "But who do you say that I am?" So what is your answer? Who do you say Jesus is?

I say Jesus is my all in all. He is my rock in a weary land, He is my sure shelter in the time of storm. He is everything I need when I need it. From A to Z, Jesus is everything to me:

A – He's Alpha and Omega

B – The Bright and Morningstar

C – The Captain of My Salvation

D – The Deliverer of My Soul

E – He's Everlasting to Everlasting

F – He's a Friend Who Sticks Closer than a Brother

G – He's Good News

H – He's Holy

I – He's Immutable

J – He's the Judge of Israel

---

[12] David. L. McKenna and Lloyd J. Ogilvie. The Preacher's Commentary(Nashville, TN: Thomas Nelson Inc, 1982), 169-172.

K – He's the King of Kings

L – He's the Lord of Lords

M – He's a Magnificent Messiah

N – He Will Never Leave You

O – He's Omnipotent, Omniscient, and Omnipresent

P – He's the Prince of Peace

Q – He's Quick and Powerful

R – He's a Righteous God

S – He's the Savior of the World

T – He's the Truth

U – He's a Universal God

V – He's the Vine, and We Are the Branches

W – He's a Way-Making God

X – He Has X-Ray Eyes

Y – It's for *You* that Jesus Died

Z – He's Zealous to Save Us and Zealous to Make Us Whole[13]

So there, I ask you once again, "Who do you say Jesus is?"
Be careful how you answer. It makes all the difference in eternity.

For Further Discussion and Reflection:

1. Why do you think Jesus waited until He and His disciples were in Caesarea Philippi before He posed the question to His disciples, "Who do men say that I am?"
2. How do their responses to the questions Jesus posed indicate the level of understanding of the disciples?
3. How can we as a church community adequately portray Jesus as the real thing?
4. How is Jesus the real thing in your life?

---

13   Broderick Huggins. Saint Paul Baptist Church, Oxnard, California, 1991, Sermon.

Chapter 10

THE PRIORITY OF PRAYER

Day 8, Thursday, September 3, 2009: Retreat Day, Jesus Cave

EXCURSION BACKGROUND

The pilgrim team was sincerely encouraged to use day 8 as a day of retreat and reflection. This was our last day in Galilee before heading to Jerusalem. There were no scheduled activities. We were asked to spend time in meditative reflection and rest throughout the day.

The day proved to be a turning point for me as it related to my toxic attitude and self-centered perspective. At this point on the journey, I was still frustrated over the lost luggage episode. My thinking was very narrow. For eight days, I had been without a complete change of clothing. Even though I kept the two outfits I had fresh through daily washing, it was an annoying experience. While the team was bonding during the evening, I was in the room, hand washing and hanging my change of clothes to dry for the next day's activities. I felt extremely discouraged because I was missing out. Thus, I was anxiously looking forward to this day of retreat and reflection.

I decided to spend time alone, praying and confronting my downward-spiraling attitude. I visited the Jesus Cave. It was not my first time visiting this traditional site, where it is said that Jesus often spent time alone, praying. My pilgrimage roommate, Steve Kurtz, had invited me to tag along with him on a few early mornings prior to this visit.

I vividly remember walking along a rocky, spiraling road to an area where there was a cave-like shelter on a hill, looking over the Sea of Galilee. Upon arriving, I sat where I thought Jesus would have sat and began to pray to God with a spirit of repentance and confession. I felt the need to tell God how sorry I was for allowing an attitude of ungratefulness to overshadow His goodness and mercy. I bowed my head and cried out to God with sincere confession.

For the first time since my arrival in the Holy Land, I felt truly grateful for the experience of walking where Jesus walked. Even though I had yet to take possession of my luggage, Jesus had already taken possession of my eternal soul, and that alone was worthy of all my thanks. The apostle Paul is right: "In everything give thanks: for this is the will of God in Christ Jesus concerning you" (1 Thess. 5:18 KJV).

Major sitting in prayerful reflection on the
Mount of Beatitudes in the Jesus Cave

Scripture Reflection: Matthew 14:22–23 KJV

And straightway Jesus constrained his disciples to
get into a ship, and to go before him unto the other
side, while he sent the multitudes away. And when
he had sent the multitudes away, he went up into a
mountain apart to pray: and when the evening was
come, he was there alone.

The Devotional

As a little boy growing up in Muskegon, I had a fascination
with birds. Being a relatively good artist in elementary school, I
would often draw birds whenever the art instructor allowed us to
draw freehand. My favorite bird of all was the American robin, the
official bird of the State of Michigan. No one in my third grade
class (Angel Elementary, Muskegon, Michigan) could draw this
bird better than me.

To this day, I love watching birds. I enjoy it because they
illustrate many wonderful things about God and the majesty of God.
For instance, birds do not die of worry and depression, because God
takes care of them. You will never see a bird in the unemployment
line, because God provides for the birds.

Birds also illustrate the power of prayer. I remember reading
somewhere, though I forget where at the moment, how birds can
fall asleep while sitting on branches, but they never fall off. This is
because of the tendons in the bird's legs. The tendons are constructed
in such a way that when the legs are bent at the knee, the claws
instinctively grip like a steel trap. The claws will not let go until the
knees are unbent again.

This is the secret of the holding power of the Christian. When
we, as Christians, bend our knees in prayer, we can hold on during
the storms of life. When we, as Christians, bend our knees in prayer,

we can walk around with joyous hearts, even while still in the fiery furnace, and not get burned. When believers bend their knees in prayer, we can rest assured, even while in a den of lions. No wonder Jesus made prayer a priority.

Notice what happens in this passage. Jesus dismissed the crowd and made the disciples get into the boat and leave. Then Jesus went alone up on a mountainside to pray. Why did Jesus dismiss His disciples and the crowd? Only because He wanted time to communicate with His Father.

During His ministry on earth, Jesus was in constant contact with the Father. Jesus continually sought strength from God. Going into the hills, away from the crowds, alone with the Father, helped Jesus focus on His task and gain strength for what He had to do.

Now, if Jesus made it His priority to spend time with the Father in prayer, then prayer should also be a priority for us. If we as a people of God are going to experience the holding power of God on a consistent basis, we need to make prayer top priority.

THE PASSION FOR PRAYER

"He went up into a mountain apart to pray." Walking up the mountain after a long day of ministering to people showed the passion Jesus had for prayer. Too often, too many of God's people do not possess adequate passion for prayer. We tend to pray only when we are overwhelmed with life's challenges.

If you are going to have success in prayer, you have to exhibit a passion for prayer prior to the occurrences of problems. Like anything else, little effort will produce little results, and significant effort will produce significant results. We need to start our days, our projects, our trips, and our work with prayer.

It is said that the child of God should PUSH, or Pray Until Something Happens. The problem is too many of us do *not* pray until something happens!

THE PLACE OF PRAYER

"A mountain apart." Jesus spent time alone to pray. Praying alone or in private does not negate public prayer, but it enhances the effectiveness of our praying.

Everyone needs a private place to engage in daily prayer. It may be your bathroom, bedroom, basement, car, office, or another secluded spot. Jesus chose to get away to a mountainside to spend time communicating with the Father. It doesn't matter where your mountainside is, so as long as you are in a private place to focus on prayer and gain strength for the task of the day.

For Further Discussion and Reflection:

1. To you, what does it mean to pray?
2. Why do you think Jesus made it His priority to "get away" and pray?
3. How can one tell that Jesus had a passion for prayer?
4. If prayer is powerful, why don't we pray more often?
5. How would you advise others to place prayer as a top priority?

Chapter 11

THE JOURNEY TO JERUSALEM

*Day 9, Friday, September 4, 2009: Galilee to
Jerusalem, Megiddo, and Caesarea Maritima*

EXCURSION BACKGROUND

Oh boy! What a day this was. We left Galilee for Jerusalem early in
the morning, though I can't remember how early. All I remember is
that the Holy Ghost had now confronted my entire attitude, and I
was filled with a brand-new sense of expectation and thankfulness.

After getting settled in the coach, the pilgrim team members
responsible for leading us in our morning devotion earlier, led us in
singing Songs of Ascent.

What are Songs of Ascent? In short, they are psalms that
were sung by Jewish worshippers as they went up to the temple in
Jerusalem for annual festivals (Deut. 16:16). Each psalm sung was
as if it were a step along the journey toward Jerusalem. There were
a total of fifteen Songs of Ascent (Psalms 120–134). They are also
called Pilgrim Psalms.

As we began our ascent to Jerusalem, I began quietly but audibly
praising and thanking God for this awesome furthering of the
experience of walking where Jesus walked.

WORSHIP IN JERUSALEM

Jewish, Christian, and Muslim pilgrims have made their way to Jerusalem through the centuries in order to worship at three spots that are surprisingly near to each other. Jews come to pray at the Wailing Wall, a remnant of the retaining wall that surrounded the Second Temple. Christian pilgrims focus their attention on visiting the Church of the Holy Sepulchre and the Garden Tomb, located near the hill called Golgotha. Muslims pray at the Dome of the Rock and al-Aksa Mosque, both within what had been the Second Temple compound.

JERUSALEM IS A CITY OF FAITH

The city of Jerusalem has witnessed events that lie near the hearts of millions of people worldwide—Jewish, Christian, and Muslim. One of the most well-known landmarks in the Old City is an Islamic shrine, the glorious Dome of the Rock. The Dome covers the Holy Rock, which in turn marks the site of the Jewish temple's Holy of Holies. The latter sanctuary contained the Ark of the Covenant. It is from here, some Muslims believe, that Muhammad flew to meet God on a winged horse. The spires and domes of scores of churches pierce the skyline, chief among them being the Church of the Holy Sepulchre. This church, atop Golgotha or Calvary, enshrines the place where we as Christians believe Jesus died on the cross and then rose again.

THE DIVISION OF THE NEW AND OLD CITIES OF JERUSALEM

There is more to Jerusalem than the Old City. The East and West Jerusalem neighborhoods have, for the most part, sprung up in the last hundred years. West Jerusalem is dynamic and teeming with energy. There are shopping centers galore and excellent westernized food. For most residents and many visitors, this is the "real" Jerusalem, the Jerusalem of today.

The Old City, with its magnificent history, serves as a reminder of the city's origins in the biblical past. Consisting of dozens of modern neighborhoods, this part is almost entirely Jewish. Jerusalem's downtown area is around Zion Square, a short distance west of the Old City.[14]

The walled Old City, the focal point for most visitors, lies close to Jerusalem's eastern edge. The Old City is informally divided into four quarters—Muslim, Christian, Armenian, and Jewish. I spent much of my personal time roaming the Old City streets of all four quarters. I was careful to take pictures of and with people in the various divisions.

As I roamed the four quarters, the division was so definitive that it reminded me of the Western Christian church, of how divided we are on Sunday mornings as a people. This ought not to be the case. Jesus died and shed His blood to reconcile us to Himself as a body of believers, not to be divided. Paul reminds us, "I appeal to you, brothers, by the name of our Lord Jesus Christ, that all of you agree, and that there be no divisions among you, but that you be united in the same mind and the same judgment" (1 Cor. 1:10 ESV).

SCRIPTURE REFLECTION: PSALM 120:1–7 KJV

In my distress I cried unto the LORD, and he heard me. Deliver my soul, O LORD, from lying lips, and from a deceitful tongue. What shall be given unto thee? or what shall be done unto thee, thou false tongue? Sharp arrows of the mighty, with coals of juniper. Woe is me, that I sojourn in Mesech, that

---

[14] Andrew Sanger. "Jerusalem", Fodor's Exploring Israel, (Random House, 2007), 49.

I dwell in the tents of Kedar! My soul hath long dwelt with him that hateth peace. I am for peace: but when I speak, they are for war.

THE DEVOTIONAL

CHOOSE TO BE A PERSON OF PEACE

Psalm 120 begins the journey of ascent to Jerusalem for the annual festivals (Passover, Pentecost, and Tabernacles). The psalmist is making a plea for relief from enemies. He is looking forward to going to Jerusalem, where he would experience an environment of peace and truth, a temporary shielding from his enemies, the Meshech and Kedar peoples, who were very hostile.

The psalmist wanted to experience peace, not fight for it. Some battles we need to let the Lord fight for us. "The LORD shall fight for you, and ye shall hold your peace" (Exod. 14:14).

As believers, we must live with the tension of being in the world but not belonging to the world (Rom. 12:2). In this world, there will always be people who will in some way make life harder for you than you deserve. There will always be those who act as if it is their lives' purpose to war against you.

The psalmist makes a wise and spiritually mature decision and says, "I am for peace" (v. 7). Even though peacemaking is not always popular, we should always, whenever possible, choose peace. When tempted to argue over who gets the last piece of chicken, choose peace. When tempted to argue about the toilet seat being left in the up position, choose peace. When someone forgets to call and cancel dinner plans for which you have spent hours preparing, choose peace. We should choose peace because peacemaking is God's way!

SCRIPTURE REFLECTION: PSALM 133:1–3

Behold, how good and how pleasant it is for brethren to dwell together in unity! It is like the precious ointment upon the head, that ran down upon the beard, even Aaron's beard: that went down to the skirts of his garments; As the dew of Hermon, and as the dew that descended upon the mountains of Zion: for there the Lord commanded the blessing, even life for evermore.

CHOOSE TO BE A PERSON OF UNITY

In this short pilgrim psalm, David remarked upon "how good and how pleasant it is" for believers to dwell together in unity. This thought was appropriate because as the people journeyed to Jerusalem, they would travel for miles and sometimes for days together in large groups. Unity was necessary for them to reach their destination safely. They could not afford to be divided as a people, because division served as a distraction on their journey. Distractions allowed would-be attackers to sneak up on those distracted and endanger them. Travelers would have been concerned about bandits and wild animals hiding out in the caves and grottos along the way.

It is a beautiful thing when unity exists in the church. Unfortunately, too many people allow disagreement to divide the church over nonessential issues. There are good reasons why unity should be top priority in the twenty-first-century church. First, unity propels ministry forward with fresh energy, because there is less tension to sap the energy of the workers. Second, unity means that cooperation is at a premium. The church needs people who will cooperate with the vision of the church in order to do effective ministry. Third, when church members operate in a spirit of unity, it makes the church a positive example to the world. It helps draw others to the church. People are not blind to disunity in the church. If it exists, others will sense it or, worse yet, see it.

PSALM 134:1–3

> Behold, bless ye the Lord, all ye servants of the Lord, which by night stand in the house of the Lord. Lift up your hands in the sanctuary, and bless the Lord. The Lord that made heaven and earth bless thee out of Zion.

CHOOSE TO BE A PERSON WHO BLESSES

The Passover, Pentecost, or Tabernacles festival is now over. Pilgrims are preparing to go home. They are singing their final hymn. Addressing the priests and the Levites whose job it is to watch over the temple, the pilgrim prays for God's blessings to be given from Zion.

This psalm teaches us to bless those who are continually ministering before the Lord on our behalf. It invites all ministers to pronounce blessings of benediction upon the people they love and for whom they pray. What a blessing it is to pray for your pastor and for your pastor to pray and pronounce a benediction upon you. The Bible teaches us to pray for *all* those in authority. Since the office of pastor or elder is the highest office in the church, God wants us to pray for our pastor. If some of us prayed for our pastors as much as we talked about them or complained about them, our personal spiritual lives and our churches would be much healthier.

However, just as it is important for us to bless our pastors, so too must our pastors be a blessing to us. The Hebrew writer encourages Pastors to "watch for your souls, as they that must give account, that they may do it with joy" (Heb. 13:17 KJV). Pastors can be a tremendous blessing to the people of God when they willingly and lovingly look out for the souls of the people.

The reciprocity of prayer between pastors and people is not always easy to do, though it is the blessed thing to do.

For Further Discussion and Reflection:

1. How were the Songs of Ascent important to the early believers as they journeyed to Jerusalem?

2. In what ways was being unified critical to the success of their journey to Jerusalem?

3. How is choosing to be a person of peace beneficial to the body of Christ?

4. In what ways can you show more unity in your local church where you serve?

5. In what ways (other than prayer) can you seek to bless your pastor?

6. What does it mean for your pastor to look out for your soul?

Chapter 12

PRESSING YOUR WAY THROUGH

*Day 10, Saturday, September 5, 2009: The
Mount of Olives, Garden of Gethsemane*

EXCURSION BACKGROUND

Day 10 was a ministry-altering day for me. We visited, among other sights, the Mount of Olives, the garden of Gethsemane, and the Church of the Holy Sepulchre (to be discussed in next chapter). Each of these sites heightened my experience of walking where Jesus walked.

The Mount of Olives and the garden of Gethsemane sites had a very profound impact upon my journey. As mentioned earlier, I was serving as the senior pastor of a church in Flint, Michigan, bearing the same name: Gethsemane Missionary Baptist Church. During that time as well, I was being considered as a candidate for senior pastor of a church bearing the name of the mountain on which I would be standing: Mount Olive Missionary Baptist Church. So to visit the two sites bearing these names about which I was in deep prayer was very thought provoking for me.

*A picture of Gethsemane Church and the Mount
of Olives, taken from Jerusalem*

The Mount of Olives was where Jesus spent nights during his last week in Jerusalem (Luke 21:37). Separated from Jerusalem by the Kidron Valley, the Mount of Olives provides an excellent view of the city from the east.

Visiting Gethsemane, which means "oil press," I was feeling pressed, constrained, and compelled to prepare for possibly transitioning to another church within the same city limits. This may not seem pressing to some, but within Flint Baptist church circles, it was very unusual. Thus, it was a situation for which much prayer was necessary.

Once we arrived at the garden of Gethsemane, I felt it both necessary and right to find a place and commence praying. Adjacent to the garden, there is a church called Gethsemane. Within the walls of the church is an enormous flat rock where, tradition says, Jesus prayed until blood-like sweat dripped from his face: "And being in an agony he prayed more earnestly: and his sweat was as it were great drops of blood falling down to the ground" (Luke 22:44).

There I fell prostrate, with both hands atop the huge, flat rock, and prayed. I prayed a prayer of surrender to God and left my entire concern about the possible transition on the surface of that stone. Even though there were many others around the rock, I was so engaged in earnest prayer that it seemed I was the only person in the room: just me and the Holy Spirit.

Major and other pilgrims praying on the same rock
upon which tradition says Jesus prayed

As I knelt on the rock, a great sense of burden and uncertainty was evident in my heart. After spending several minutes in solitude and prayer, the Spirit of God began ministering to me in a powerful and transformative way. My burdens became noticeably lighter, and my vision for ministry became much clearer.

When I stood on my feet, I knew within my heart that the Holy Spirit, once again, had positively altered my perspective. On that day, there in Gethsemane, the Holy Spirit ministered to me that I should not look at this possible transition as leaving one church and going to another church. That was too narrow a vision. Rather, this was an elevation move assigned by God. It was not a promotion from one church to another, but merely another opportunity to prepare me to do ministry in a different context, all within the kingdom of God.

How would this be an elevation move? Gethsemane is physically located almost at the foot of the Mount of Olives. To get to the groves on the mountain, one must go up. I believe the Spirit of God impressed upon me in a unique way that transitioning from Gethsemane Baptist Church to Mt. Olive Baptist Church was an elevation move. It was going up—not in the sense that one church was better than the other, but in the sense that God had used my experiences at Gethsemane Baptist Church to help prepare me for the pastoral assignment at Mt Olive Baptist Church.

It is important to remember that God has a plan and purpose for the life of the pastor as well as for the people of God. God desires pastors to become more in the likeness of Jesus Christ, just as He desires that for every Christian. As God uses life experiences to shape and sharpen laity, He does the same for pastors.

In Romans 8:29, Paul writes, "For whom he did foreknow, he also did predestinate to be conformed to the image of his Son, that he might be the firstborn among many brethren" (KJV). Born-again believers are predestined, marked out, appointed, or determined beforehand. The goal of God's predestined purpose is that believers become more and more like Jesus Christ.

This move, this elevation, was part of God's plan, which was predetermined or marked out, to help me conform more closely to the image of Jesus Christ. The transition experiences I had while moving my ministry from Gethsemane Baptist Church to Mt. Olive Baptist Church helped develop my level of spiritual maturity at a rapid rate. I quickly learned who my genuine friends were. I discovered that my hope truly is built on nothing less than Jesus's blood and righteousness. Oh, how quickly I learned.

Major standing in the garden of Gethsemane

SCRIPTURE REFLECTIONS: LUKE 22:39–46 KJV

And he came out, and went, as he was wont, to the Mount of Olives, and his disciples also followed him. And when he was at the place, he said unto them, Pray that ye enter not into temptation. And he was withdrawn from them about a stone's cast, and kneeled down, and prayed, Saying, Father, if thou be willing, remove this cup from me: nevertheless not my will, but thine, be done. And there appeared an angel unto him from heaven, strengthening him. And being in an agony he prayed more earnestly: and his sweat was as it were great drops of blood falling down to the ground. And when he rose up from prayer, and was come to his disciples, he found them sleeping for sorrow, And said unto them, Why sleep ye? rise and pray, lest ye enter into temptation.

THE DEVOTIONAL

What a vivid picture of Jesus praying to His Father as He pressed His way through His ordeal. In this prayer, the Lord teaches the Christian a very important lesson about pressing or persevering through times of difficulties.

WE MUST RESIST TEMPTATION AS WE PRESS

"Enter not into temptation" (v. 40). Leaning and depending solely on God is the key to successfully resisting temptations while in the midst of our struggles. Scripture promises, "There hath no temptation taken you but such as is common to man: but God is faithful, who will not suffer you to be tempted above that ye are able; but will with the temptation also make a way to escape, that ye may be able to bear it" (1 Cor. 10:13).

The people of God are all different. We are different in terms of our body shapes, sizes, and colors. We come from different parts of the world, country, state, or city. However, one thing that makes all of us alike is temptation. All of us will be tempted on occasion. The blessing is that, with each temptation, God has an escape route.

Not only is temptation common to the Christian, but so is trouble. We all will experience trouble from time to time. Scripture bears witness that trouble does not discriminate. In the book of James, it says, "My brethren, count it all joy when ye fall into divers temptations" (1:2). We have all been lied on. We have all been the innocent parties of half-truths and innuendos.

A friend of mine, Rev. E. Thomas Baker, is known for his "Truth Moment" on the social media platform called Facebook. He sometimes write about a life issue that everyone knows is typically true, but no one has the audacity to write about except for Baker! Well, I have a "Truth Moment" to share. The truth is, we cannot get through life without trouble. No matter what we do to avoid trouble,

trouble will eventually make its way into our lives. And when it shows up, we must be ready to confront it with godly wisdom.

Even though we will experience temptations in life, the blessing is that all temptations are under God's control. In other words, because God is faithful, we need not worry about what temptations may come our way. God is with us and He will see us through.

We may face financial difficulty, but God is faithful. We may have to experience a sickness of some sort, but God is faithful. No matter what happens to us, God remains faithful. When the sun is shining, God is faithful. When there are rain clouds in the sky, God is faithful. God is faithful to His Word. He will never let us down.

God may allow us to go into the fire, but He will definitely bring us through the fire. Burdens may seem unbearable, but God will never allow the weight of the burden to be more than we can bear. Isaiah says, "When thou passest through the waters, I will be with thee; and through the rivers, they shall not overflow thee: when thou walkest through the fire, thou shalt not be burned; neither shall the flame kindle upon thee" (43:2). Whatever our temptation, whatever our trouble, whatever our trial, God will see us through!

For Further Discussion and Reflection:

1. Have you ever experienced a Gethsemane "oil press" situation? How did you handle it?
2. To you, what does it mean to submit to the will of God?
3. Why do you think it is important to resist temptation when seeking to press your way through a trying situation?
4. How are temptations common to all people?
5. What advice can you give to someone who is struggling with a seemingly overwhelming temptation?

Chapter 13

THE VIA DOLOROSA

*Day 10 continued, Saturday, September 5,
2009: Church of the Holy Sepulchre*

EXCURSION BACKGROUND

On the tenth day, we also spent a considerable amount of time at the
Church of the Holy Sepulchre, also called the Basilica of the Holy
Sepulchre or the Church of the Resurrection by Eastern Christians.
This church is located within the Old City of Jerusalem. As I recall,
it was around midday Saturday, with crowded streets full of tourists
and people from the Old City. The Church of the Holy Sepulchre
was very crowded as well.

The church is acclaimed as Calvary (Golgotha) by some
Christians, where Jesus was crucified, and also contains the place
where Jesus is said to have been buried. Within the church are the
last four (or, by some definitions, five) stations of the cross along
the Via Dolorosa, representing the final episodes of Jesus's passion.
The church has been an important Christian pilgrimage destination
since at least the fourth century as the alleged site of the resurrection
of Jesus.

People were lined up, standing around, and anxiously waiting
for an opportunity to see and experience the tomb where Jesus once

lay. Interestingly enough, in order to see the tomb, there was a very low doorway to enter. The only way in, as I recall, was to stoop with your knees bent.

As I reflect on how I had to stoop positionally before entering the tomb, I could not help thinking about how we as Christians must be in a similar position spiritually before coming into the presence of God. We must stoop with humility because "God resisteth the proud, but giveth grace unto the humble" (James 4:6). We must stoop with reverence because God told Moses, "Draw not nigh hither: put off thy shoes from off thy feet, for the place whereon thou standest [is] holy ground" (Exod. 3:5). We must stoop with thanksgiving because "in everything give thanks: for this is the will of God in Christ Jesus concerning you" (1 Thess. 5:18).

Major and another pilgrim entering through a very low doorway leading to the tomb chamber of Jesus

Today, the Church of the Holy Sepulchre also serves as the headquarters of the Greek Orthodox Patriarch of Jerusalem. Control of the building has been shared among several Christian churches and secular entities for centuries. Anglicans and Protestants have no permanent presence in the church.

Some people believe the Garden Tomb is located somewhere else in Jerusalem, as the actual place of the crucifixion and resurrection of Jesus Christ (addressed in a later chapter).

VIA DOLOROSA AND THE STATIONS OF THE CROSS

The Via Dolorosa (Latin, "Way of Sorrow," "Way of Sorrows," "Way of Suffering" or simply "Painful Way") is a street within the Old City of Jerusalem. It is held to be the path that Jesus walked, carrying His cross, on the way to His crucifixion and, ultimately, His bodily resurrection from the dead three days later.

The winding route from the Antonia Fortress west to the Church of the Holy Sepulchre—a distance of about 2,000 feet or 666 yards—is a celebrated place of Christian pilgrimage. The current route has been established since the eighteenth century, replacing various earlier versions. Today the route is marked by nine stations of the cross, with the remaining five stations being inside the church.

*The fifth station of the Via Dolorosa, where
Simon helps Jesus carry the cross*

*The seventh station of the Via Dolorosa, where Jesus
falls again under the weight of the cross*

Scripture Reflection: Matthew 27:31–35 KJV

And after that they had mocked him, they took the robe off from him, and put his own raiment on him, and led him away to crucify him. And as they came out, they found a man of Cyrene, Simon by name: him they compelled to bear his cross. And when they were come unto a place called Golgotha, that is to say, a place of a skull, They gave him vinegar to drink mingled with gall: and when he had tasted thereof, he would not drink. And they crucified him.

The Devotional

Most Christian communities take the view that Christ's suffering was spiritual and symbolic as well as physical, and it is not essential to know the actual route Jesus followed. However, tens of thousands of pilgrims of all denominations walk the Via Dolorosa each year, all of whom believe in the spirit that, in fact, they are stepping in Christ's footsteps as He made His way to Calvary's cross to die for the sins of the world.

As I walked along this path from shrine to shrine, at some point I became emotionally overwhelmed. My entire body began to shake physically with a great sense of thankfulness. What a mighty God we serve. For Him to love us so, to walk through the streets of shame, hate, and sin—the Via Dolorosa—determined to die for you and me.

THE 14 STATIONS OF THE CROSS ON THE VIA DOLOROSA

Station 1. *Condemnation*: The first part of the way is relatively wide and quiet. The first station is the courtyard of the Omariye Islamic College, which some claim as the site where Jesus was condemned and sentenced.

Station 2. *Taking Up the Cross*: Across the street, the ancient paving in the Franciscan Churches of the Condemnation is said to be where Jesus was mocked, crowned with thorns, and given His cross to carry. Condemned prisoners had to carry their own crosses all the way to the place where the crucifixion was to take place.

Station 3. *Jesus Falls*: Here a plaque shows where Jesus fell under the weight of the cross.

Station 4. *Meeting Mary*: On the left, a shrine marks the place where tradition claims that Jesus saw His mother.

Station 5. *Simon Helps Jesus*: Here, a bystander by the name of Simon the Cyrenian helped Jesus to carry His cross. Simon was from Africa and was probably in Jerusalem for the Passover festivities.

Station 6. *Veronica Wipes the Face of Jesus*: The story that a woman named Veronica wiped the face of Jesus arose in the seventh century.

Station 7. *Jesus Falls Again*: The route reaches a junction in the midst of crowded shopping streets, where tradition holds that Jesus fell again.

Station 8. *Speaking to the Women*: Here Jesus urged the women of Jerusalem to weep not for Him but for themselves and their children.

Station 9. *Jesus Falls Again*: Here believers say Jesus fell a third time.

Station 10. *Jesus Stripped*: At the door of the Church of the Holy Sepulchre.

Station 11. *Jesus Is Nailed to the Cross*: At the altar within the Church of the Holy Sepulchre.

Station 12. *The Cross Is Raised and Jesus Dies*: The crucifixion.

Station 13. *Jesus Removed from the Cross.*

Station 14. *Jesus Is Entombed and Returns to Life*: Here there is a small doorway into the narrow marble-clad burial chamber, the place where the body of Jesus is claimed to have lain.[15]

For Further Discussion and Reflection:

1. The Garden Tomb and the Church of the Holy Sepulchre are the two places where it is purported that the death, burial, and resurrection of Jesus Christ occurred. What difference does it make to you to know where Jesus's crucifixion took place?
2. What is the significance of the fourteen stations of the cross?
3. What is the significance of the Via Dolorosa?
4. What does it mean to be humble in His presence?

—

[15] Andrew Sanger. "Via Dolorosa", Fodor's Exploring Israel. (Random House, Inc. 2007), 76-77.

Chapter 14

JESUS IS THE GOOD SHEPHERD

*Day 11, Sunday, September 6, 2009: Worship in
Bethlehem, Palestinian Refugee Camp*

EXCURSION BACKGROUND

On Day 11, we visited Bethlehem, Palestine, which is about six miles
from Jerusalem. The Hebrew name for Bethlehem means "House
of Bread." I think it is fitting that the Bread of Life was born in the
House of Bread (John 6:35).

It was a day of epic joy for me because we were going to visit the
birthplace of my Savior and spend Sunday morning worshipping my
Lord at a Lutheran Palestinian church in Bethlehem. The church
service was an awesome experience as we worshipped with Arab
Christians. I experienced a significant presence of the Spirit of
God flowing throughout the church as we sang and the minister
preached. It was a wonderful and memorable experience. After the
worship service, we had an opportunity to eat lunch and fellowship
with some of the leaders of the church.

As I recall, this was the first day where I felt totally and utterly
at peace with myself and with what I sensed God was doing in my
life. I do not believe it was anything that was preached or even said
to me by someone else. It was not in the songs we sang. I know it

was definitely a God thing, where my spirit was in final agreement with God's Spirit. No more wrestling with God for a special blessing, because the realization of the blessing has now arrived. On that day, at some point during that worship service, the Spirit of God stood up within my soul, victorious, as my self-centered perspective tapped out in surrender to God's will and way. I was finally free.

After lunch, we visited the Dheisheh Refugee Camp. This Palestinian camp is located just south of Bethlehem in the West Bank. It was established in 1949 as a temporary refuge for 3,400 Palestinians from forty-five villages west of Jerusalem and Hebron who fled during the 1948 Arab-Israeli War. Although initially living in tents, the residents have since constructed homes. Many streets are now paved while still remaining very narrow.[16]

As our daily transportation, the motor coach, navigated through security checkpoints, I remember experiencing personal fear for some unknown reason. To this day, I cannot quite explain why I felt as I did. I do not know if it was the guns carried by the guards at the various points of entry. I just do not know.

What I do know is, for the very first time during my pilgrimage journey of walking where Jesus walked, I found myself wrestling with something other than my faith. Now it was fear. Here I was, in Bethlehem, the House of Bread, where the Bread of Life was born, where Jesus the Good Shepherd was born, with unknown fear in my heart. I remember thinking, "I will be glad when this part of the journey is over."

I now regret having those thoughts, because God did not give us the spirit of fear (2 Tim. 1:7). I realize whatever fear I was experiencing was not of God and came from another place. Perhaps I was relying on man's reports of various kidnappings, rather than trusting the protection and power of the Lord to overrule the attempt of the Enemy to steal my new freedom and joy.

---

[16] Wikipedia. "Dheisheh", April 15, 2013, Web. January 10, 2015

We also visited the Church of the Nativity in Manger Square, known to the world as the birthplace of Jesus. The church is built over a grotto where the Virgin Mary is said to have given birth to Jesus.

In chapter 13, "The Via Dolorosa," I mentioned that one must go through a very low door to enter the tomb of Jesus. In the Church of the Nativity, there is another small door one must enter to see the birthplace of our Lord and Savior. This small door is called the Door of Humility. In both churches, stooping is required. Whether one enters through the Door of Humility or any other door in God's house, we should approach Jesus and God's throne of grace with a sincere spirit of stooping in humility.

Far too many occasions take place in the church when people do, act, or say whatever they feel. This behavior is not of God. As Christians, we should not behave offensively or disrespectfully in the house of the Lord. Our behavior should exemplify stooping and not stupidity. Our approach before God's throne should be one of humility because "God resisteth the proud, but giveth grace unto the humble" (James 4:6).

The Church of Nativity, a pilgrim stooping at the Door of Humility

SCRIPTURE REFLECTION: JOHN 10:7–18 KJV

Then said Jesus unto them again, Verily, verily, I say unto you, I am the door of the sheep. All that ever came before me are thieves and robbers: but the sheep did not hear them. I am the door: by me if any man enter in, he shall be saved, and shall go in and out, and find pasture. The thief cometh not, but for to steal, and to kill, and to destroy: I am come that they might have life, and that they might have it more abundantly. I am the good shepherd: the good shepherd giveth his life for the sheep. But he that is an hireling, and not the shepherd, whose own the sheep are not, seeth the wolf coming, and leaveth the sheep, and fleeth: and the wolf catcheth them, and scattereth the sheep. The hireling fleeth, because he is an hireling, and careth not for the sheep. I am the good shepherd, and know my sheep, and am known of mine. As the Father knoweth me, even so know I the Father: and I lay down my life for the sheep.

And other sheep I have, which are not of this fold: them also I must bring, and they shall hear my voice; and there shall be one fold, and one shepherd. Therefore doth my Father love me, because I lay down my life, that I might take it again. No man taketh it from me, but I lay it down of myself. I have power to lay it down, and I have power to take it again. This commandment have I received of my Father.

THE DEVOTIONAL

A few years ago, I heard a story about two men who were invited to recite the Twenty-third Psalm in a large auditorium full of people. One man was a great and well-known public speaker who was also a professional actor. He quoted the psalm in a very powerful and articulate manner. Afterward, the crowd gave him a standing ovation and wanted to hear him again.

Then the other man, who was elderly, recited the same psalm. When he finished, the crowd did not give him a standing ovation. Instead, just about every person either cried or sat in deep devotion and contemplation.

Then the well-known public speaker got up from his seat and said, "I have something I need to say to you all today. There is a major difference between what you have heard from the both of us. I know the psalm, but the old man knows the Shepherd!"

The passage from John reminds us how blessed we are to have Jesus as our Good Shepherd. As our Shepherd, Jesus is concerned about His sheep. He is concerned about our eternal spiritual affairs. Jesus does not just save us and send us out to make our own way. Rather, Jesus continues to show concern and love for us as we journey through life. That's an amazing thought! We are blessed beyond measure to have such a gracious Shepherd to follow. Notice what we have in Him.

WE HAVE ACCESS TO HEAVEN THROUGH THE GOOD SHEPHERD

"I am the door of the sheep" (v.7). Jesus proclaims that He is the only means of entrance into the sheepfold. In other words, the only way anyone can go to heaven is by going through Jesus Christ. Jesus told His disciples, "I am the way, the truth, and the life: no man cometh unto the Father, but by me" (John 14:6).

Jesus was not speaking of a door like the ones that are familiar to us. In His day, sheep were typically enclosed by a stone wall. An opening was left for an entrance. The shepherd became the door of the sheepfold as he lay between the door posts. He was literally their door, their defense, and their umbrella of protection. The only way an intruder could gain entrance was to go through the shepherd. Jesus is saying that no thief or robber is going to be successful in stealing or destroying His sheep. Amen!

WE HAVE ABUNDANT LIFE THROUGH THE GOOD SHEPHERD

"I am come that they might have life, and that they might have it more abundantly" (v. 10). Others sought to steal and destroy, but Jesus promised to provide an abundant and full life to the sheep. Jesus was on a very important mission. His mission was to die on the cross so that we could have eternal life. Jesus came to give us life more abundantly. He came to give us a life of victory, a life of joy and peace. This is the abundant life! It is not the ordinary life for the Christian to be living below the poverty line of victory, joy, and peace. Instead, the life of Christians ought to mirror the abundance of His grace, mercy, and favor. The Christian is supposed to be living life in the overflow of victory, joy and peace!

When I think of the abundant life Jesus offers us, I cannot help but think about the cup discussed in Psalm 23:5: "Thou preparest a table before me in the presence of mine enemies: thou anointest my head with oil; my cup runneth over" (KJV). The psalmist describes a host who cares enough to pour into his thirsty and honored guest's cup until it overflows.

The abundant life is the life that Jesus offers us today. The question is, are you thirsty, my friend?

For Further Discussion and Reflection:

1. How is Jesus our Good Shepherd?
2. What does it mean for Jesus to be our Good Shepherd?
3. How can we as Christians show our Good Shepherd that we are grateful for His protection?
4. Can you remember when you accepted Christ as the Shepherd of your soul?
5. What are some ways believers can continue to follow the Shepherd of our souls?
6. What are some ways believers tend to wander away from the protection of our Shepherd?

Chapter 15

HE IS NOT HERE, FOR HE IS RISEN

Day 12, Monday, September 7, 2009: Garden Tomb,
City of David, Upper Room, Mount Zion

EXCURSION BACKGROUND

Oh my! "This is it. This is the day I have been waiting for since my arrival in Israel," I kept saying to myself. This was the day the pilgrimage team would go to the Garden Tomb! Even though there were other stops along the way, our primary destination was the Garden Tomb. This is the other "accepted" burial and resurrection place of Jesus Christ.

Major standing outside the Garden Tomb of Jesus

There is an alternative site of the burial and resurrection of Jesus to the Church of the Holy Sepulchre. This so-called Garden Tomb was chosen by British General Charles Gordon in 1883 and has been acknowledged by several Protestant denominations.

Gordon was concerned that the accepted site, inside the Church of the Holy Sepulchre, stood within the city walls, in contradiction to the gospels. In fact, the city walls at the time of Christ took a different course, and the Holy Sepulchre does lie outside those walls.

Very near the Garden Tomb, there is a hill that looks like a skull (the gospel description of Golgotha), has a fine rock-hewn burial tomb adjacent, and is in a garden location. Other high-quality rock-cut tombs found nearby—for example, the Tombs of the Kings—suggest that this was a burial area preferred by the wealthy. Christ was laid in the tomb of Joseph, a rich man of Arimathaea.[17]

---

[17]   Andrew Sanger. "Garden Tomb", Fodor's Exploring Israel (Random House, Inc. 2007), 86.

A hill called Golgotha

When we arrived at the Garden Tomb, I remember feeling hyperexcited. This was the part of the trip for which I had been waiting since early 2001, while a bible student at Michigan Theological Seminary, Plymouth, Michigan (now Moody Theological Seminary). Yes, the other sites were just as significant to me, but on a comparative basis, this site was most anticipated. To be clear, every place we visited where Jesus walked had profound and lasting effects upon me. But this site represented the conquering power of the resurrection of Jesus Christ. This site was the symbol of the greatest defeat over death in all of world history. This was it!

I was in awe. I was ecstatic. I felt very close to God at that moment in time. There were many groups visiting the Garden Tomb that day. I can't remember how many, but perhaps hundreds of people moved in and out of the garden, which is a park. Many of the groups were sectioned off in different areas of the garden and held private worship services. Some groups worshipped audibly enough that singing, preaching, crying, and celebrating could be heard from where we were gathered. I have been part of many worship services in my lifetime, but none as spiritual as this. Oh, what beautiful worship I experienced. We sang in the garden, we prayed in the garden, we shared Communion in the garden, we worshipped in the garden. I remember asking myself, "Isn't this how it is supposed to be in our churches on Sunday mornings?" Well, isn't it?

Tammy Jo leading worship as we participated in Communion service in the Garden Tomb

Major and pilgrims fellowshipping after Communion service in the Garden Tomb

Still to this day, I am unable to verbalize the beauty of hearing other pilgrims worshipping and singing in their native tongues. It reminded me of the day of Pentecost in Acts 2:1 and following:

> And when the day of Pentecost was fully come, they were all with one accord in one place. And suddenly there came a sound from heaven as of a rushing mighty wind, and it filled all the house where they were sitting. And there appeared unto them cloven tongues like as of fire, and it sat upon each of them. And they were all filled with the Holy Ghost and began to speak with other tongues, as the Spirit gave them utterance. And there were dwelling at Jerusalem Jews, devout men, out of every nation under heaven. (KJV)

Did you see what I saw while reading this? There is a pattern established. When the day of Pentecost arrived—the day God poured out the Holy Spirit upon his first followers, thus empowering them for their mission and gathering them together as a church—all of God's followers were in *one accord*. They were all in *one place*. The Holy Spirit filled *all the house* where they were gathered.

In other words, there was unity of worship, unity of spirit, and unity of purpose in the church. I experienced that unity for the first time in a long time at the Garden Tomb. It was amazing!

SCRIPTURE REFLECTION: MATTHEW 28:1–10 KJV

> In the end of the sabbath, as it began to dawn toward the first day of the week, came Mary Magdalene and the other Mary to see the sepulcher. And, behold, there was a great earthquake: for the angel of the Lord descended from heaven, and came and rolled

back the stone from the door, and sat upon it. His countenance was like lightning, and his raiment white as snow: And for fear of him the keepers did shake, and became as dead men. And the angel answered and said unto the women, Fear not ye: for I know that ye seek Jesus, which was crucified. He is not here: for he is risen, as he said. Come, see the place where the Lord lay. And go quickly, and tell his disciples that he is risen from the dead; and, behold, he goeth before you into Galilee; there shall ye see him: lo, I have told you. And they departed quickly from the sepulcher with fear and great joy; and did run to bring his disciples word. And as they went to tell his disciples, behold, Jesus met them, saying, All hail. And they came and held him by the feet, and worshiped him. Then said Jesus unto them, Be not afraid: go tell my brethren that they go into Galilee, and there shall they see me.

THE DEVOTIONAL

Jesus came to earth with a purpose. He came to die for the sins of humanity. I am thankful to God Almighty for the death experience of His only begotten Son, Jesus Christ. If Jesus had not suffered, bled, and died on of the cross, there would have been no payment for our sins. Had Jesus not died, we would not have been offered life.

The good news is that Jesus's death was not the end of the story. Had His death been the end, we would have no hope for today. As a matter of fact, if Jesus had not risen from the grave, He would have been like all other men who have died before Him and have died after Him. His resurrection sets Him apart from all who came before Him. The fact of His resurrection is what gives us hope and eternal life. His resurrection is the central fact of Christianity. Because of His resurrection, we can thankfully proclaim, "He is not here: for He is risen"!

Major exiting the Tomb of Jesus. Notice the sign

A DAY OF SHAKING

It was early Sunday morning, the first day of the week, when Mary Magdalene and the other Mary came running to the grave site where Jesus had been buried the day He died. The other gospels speak of them bringing spices to anoint the body. They were expecting to find the Lord still in the grave.

As the women made their way that morning, there was an earthquake. The text says that it was a "great" earthquake. I lived in southern California for a number of years, and I personally know about "great" earthquakes. I think those experiences are partially why I am living in Michigan today. An earthquake occurs when there is a sudden and violent release of energy in the crust of the earth. Earthquakes are normally brief but often will repeat over a lengthy period of time.

This earthquake, this tremor, was not a small earthquake but a "great" earthquake. The word *great* means "violent." It was so great that it was on the Richter scale of being violent. It was so great that it shook the foundation of the earth. When that happened, perhaps even the sealing circular stone (weighing several tons) came loose from the tomb of Jesus, making it possible for the angel to roll it away.

As the women ran and maybe even walked closer to the grave, I am sure they experienced a trembling and shaking. Perhaps everything in the immediate area was disrupted, including buildings and homes. It was a major shakeup! God was "shaking up things" in Jerusalem.[18]

God is known to have used earthquakes to shake things up. In 1 Kings 19:9–18, an earthquake was the result of God passing by a depressed and suicidal Elijah on a mountain. In Acts 16:26, an earthquake shook up the prison cell of Paul and Silas, setting them free. In Matthew 27:51–54, an earthquake was accompanied by darkness, the tearing in two of the veil in the temple, and dead people rising from their tombs.

Why did God use the violence of earthquakes in these instances? I believe God was trying to get people's attention! He wanted Elijah to recognize that He is still God. He needed Paul and Silas to know that, even though the earthquake meant disaster for the prison system and officials, it meant deliverance for them. The earthquake surrounding the events of Christ's death was to let everybody know that something with eternal significance was happening on Golgotha, and somebody needed to take notice. When the Lord

---

[18] The thought of "shaking up things" came from a devotional message given by Pastor Cynthia Davis, Pilgrim 2009, during devotional period on Monday, September 7, 2009, Jerusalem.

sends spiritual earthquakes into our space, into our lives, we should listen with a sense of urgency. Are you listening?

Let's be very clear about something. The rolling away of the stone was not for the purpose of letting Jesus out of the grave. Rather, it was for Mary Magdalene and others to gain entrance into the tomb to personally see that Jesus was no longer in it.

As I reflect back over my life, especially since my journey to the Holy Land, God has repeatedly used what seemingly were "unpleasant events" as shaking experiences to the ultimate end of Him being glorified. The Lord has brought me through a number of shaking experiences, including health issues, the death of loved ones, and financial disasters, just to name a few.

But the Scripture bears witness, "Whoever serves must do so with the strength that God supplies, so that God may be glorified in all things through Jesus Christ. To him belong the glory and the power forever and ever. Amen" (1 Pet. 4:11 NRSV). God may have been trying to get my undivided attention, so that I could surely experience the resurrection power of Jesus in a new, relevant, and powerful way.

Paul says that all things work together for our good (Rom. 8:28). The loss of my luggage while in Israel was a shaking experience for me. It shook me in the sense that I became utterly helpless and did not know what to do. I had to grow to the point of trusting only in God for the eventual return of my luggage. Looking back, I needed that divine shake-up.

First of all, that particular unpleasant experience stripped me of something more important than my luggage. It brought to the forefront the urgency of dealing with an unbearable attitude. The luggage and the personal items in it, such as clothes, underclothes, walking shoes, hygiene items, and my favorite pair of jeans, were material possessions that gave me a false sense of comfort and security. The unpleasant experience stripped those things away, setting the stage for God to become the audience of one. I was stripped of more than just physical luggage. There was evident spiritual baggage I was carrying around that needed stripping too. It was all a shaking experience!

If we look at it rightly, the stripping process is a good thing. It may not feel good, but the results can be magnificent. By the time my Holy Land journey brought me to the Garden Tomb, I was indeed ready, stripped of negative attitude and lack of focus, to worship a risen Savior.

A DAY OF WORSHIP

"And they came and held him by the feet, and worshipped him" (v. 9b). As the women ran from the tomb, on their way to obediently deliver the message that Jesus had risen from the grave, they met Jesus. The women lay prostrate, holding His feet and worshipping Jesus as King of Kings and Lord of Lords. They did not worship the disciples. They did not worship the Roman soldiers. They worshipped Jesus Christ, our Savior and Lord!

Brothers and sisters, when we meet Jesus along the road of obedience, our first response will be to worship the Lord. Jesus is worthy of our worship every day, and especially on Sunday mornings, when we assemble to celebrate His resurrection. We cannot allow things, circumstances, or situations stop us from making it to the Garden Tomb of worship. We must worship Him in spirit and in truth.

Let everything that has breath praise the Lord. If you woke up this morning and are reading this book, that means you have breath. Thus, you ought to recognize the necessity of praising the Lord. So I ask you again, Isn't this how it is supposed to be in our churches on Sunday mornings? Well, isn't it?

When we left the Garden Tomb that day, I left a different man than when I came. I left with a greater appreciation for diversity in worship. There were people of many different nationalities and speaking a number of different languages. I left with a greater appreciation for other pastors who serve our Savior in various denominations, both male and female. Christians can look very different from one another, and they can hold widely varying beliefs about politics, lifestyle, and even theology. But one central belief unites and inspires all true Christians—Jesus Christ rose from the dead!

For Further Discussion and Reflection:

1. In verse 2 we see the earth shaking, and in verse 4 we find the guards shaking. Is there a message in this for us today?
2. What is the significance of the resurrection of Jesus Christ to you?
3. Why did the women rush to the grave site of Jesus so early in the morning?
4. Why is being an effective witness for Jesus Christ so vitally important for Christians today?
5. How can the twenty-first-century church do a better job of worshipping our Lord and Savior?
6. What was the true cause of surprise for the women who found the tomb empty?
7. How has Jesus resurrected your life or ministry?

Chapter 16

THE LORD IS MY SHEPHERD

*Day 13, Tuesday, September 7, 2009: Dead
Sea, Masada, Bedouin Shepherds*

EXCURSION BACKGROUND

It was an exhilarating day. Our plans as a group included visiting the Dead Sea and then going on a tour of the Masada. I was very much looking forward to both destinations.

The entire group seemed to be excited about floating in the therapeutic waters of the Dead Sea. I wanted desperately to get into the salt water for what some say is a healing experience. However, I did not want to risk breaking out with some rash or skin condition that would prevent me from enjoying the balance of my time in Israel. It had only been a few days since I had retrieved my luggage successfully. I no longer wanted to do anything to spoil the balance of my stay, so I enjoyed the Dead Sea from the shore.

THE DEAD SEA

The Dead Sea is an inland lake at the end of the Jordan Valley, on the southeastern border of Canaan, with no outlet for the water it receives. It is also known as Salt Sea, Sea of the Plain, and Eastern Sea. The current English name was applied to it after AD 100. The Dead Sea is about fifty miles long and ten miles wide at its widest point. The surface is 1,292 feet below the level of the Mediterranean Sea. At its deepest point, the lake is 1,300 feet deep. At its most shallow, it is only 10 to 15 feet deep.

The primary source of water for the sea is the Jordan River, but other, smaller rivers empty into the Dead Sea also. The Jordan River empties an average of six million tons of water into the sea every 24 hours. Despite the influx of water, the surface does not rise more than fifteen feet. Since the Dead Sea lies below sea level, the heat and aridity of its location contribute to the rapid evaporation of the water.

This, plus other geographical factors, gives it a salt content which is approximately five times the concentration of the ocean. This makes the body of water one of the world's saltiest. The Dead Sea's high salt content makes it virtually impossible for a person to sink into its waters. The salt also means no form of marine life can live there, although some fish have reportedly been found in a few of the adjacent salty pools. The surrounding land area can, however, support vegetation and life.

These features of the Dead Sea, as well as its location in a hot and arid area, inspired the biblical writers to use it as an example of life apart from the law of God.[19]

THE HEALTHIEST

The mineral-rich waters, together with hot springs, have given rise to a number of thriving spa resorts. These are nothing new: Cleopatra, Herod, and Solomon all visited the Dead Sea for a cure.

---

[19] Bob Sheffield. Holman Illustrated Bible Dictionary, ed. Chad Brand, Charles Draper, Archie England (Nashville: Holman Bible Publishers, 2003), s.v. "DEAD SEA,"

The naturally warm spring waters are a proven help in the treatment of skin and rheumatic problems. It is claimed that the water is beneficial even to healthy skin. Be careful, though, when taking a dip: the salts are painful to the eyes, lips, and mucous membranes. After bathing, the skin feels oily. Unless you are on a mission for a cure, it is far more enjoyable to swim in a hotel pool. However, a bonus is this arid zone is almost wholly pollen-free, giving relief to people with hay fever or respiratory complaints.[20]

THE MASADA

We then drove into the Judean wilderness to Herod's fortress of Masada. A ruined mountaintop fortress in the desert, overlooking the Dead Sea, Masada (pronounced Matzada) has become a potent symbol for the state and people of Israel. Israeli soldiers are sworn in here with the words, "Masada shall not fall again."

A cable car taking people to the Masada

---

[20] Andrew Sanger. "The Dead Sea", Fodor's Exploring Israel, (Random House, Inc. 2008), 230

REACHING THE SITE

From the parking areas, visitors climb dusty Snake Path to the mountaintop; the walk takes about an hour. We however, ascended by a cable car, a marvelous ride with magnificent views, leaving but eighty steps to be climbed to the site entrance.

HISTORY OF THE MASADA

The small Hasmonean fort at Masada assumed its present form under King Herod (40–4 BC), who constructed the palaces and fortifications as a desert retreat. He did not make use of it, but a Roman garrison was always stationed there. In AD 66, the knife-bearing Sicari, or Zealots, captured Masada from the Romans at the start of the First Jewish Revolt (AD 66–73). As the revolt was put down in other parts of the country, Zealots made their way here.

Eventually the Romans besieged Masada with 15,000 men. Traces of their camps can be seen at the foot of the mountain. The Zealots and their families numbered about 967. The Romans built a ramp up the western side of the mountain and breached the wall on the first day of Passover in AD 73. They found everyone dead, except for one woman and her children. She explained to them that when defeat seemed inevitable, the Zealot leader made a rousing speech, praising death above defeat and dishonor. Ten men were selected by lot to kill everyone else. Every family group lay down and were killed. Finally, the ten men killed each other, the last man killing himself. She alone decided to live.[21]

The Romans occupied Masada again briefly. Byzantine monks resided in Masada during the fifth and sixth centuries, after which the site was abandoned.

---

[21] Andrew Sanger. "Masada National Park", Fodor's Exploring Israel (Random House, Inc. 2007), 242.

The Shepherds—Bedouin

The Bedouins come from a variety of origins. The majority of Bedouin in Israel, approximately 160,000, live in the Negev, with another 70,000 in Galilee. About half of Israel's Bedouin originate in tribes which emerged from the Arabian Desert in the seventh century. They eventually migrated north to the Negev by way of the Sinai Peninsula, or to Galilee by way of Iraq and Syria.

Others are divided into two groups: farmers from Egypt and Sinai, who came north during later Turkish times, and tribes people from Sudan who arrived in the nineteenth century as slaves.[22]

The Bedouins' livelihood once depended entirely on moving their flocks through the desert from well to well and from pasture to pasture. Now, most have settled down permanently. However, among the elements of the Bedouin culture still powerfully evident from those days are extreme hospitality and close ties to family, tribe, and confederation.

The lifestyle of the Bedouin shepherds is a very interesting one. They graze their livestock in an area in Israel until it is used up, and then they pack up everything and move to a new location. The Bedouin habit is to rise early, with each family member assigned a task. They do their duties throughout the day, such as mending the tents, making clothes, shepherding the flocks, or going to town to barter their goods. Everyone pitches in, and everyone works. At the end of the day, the family comes back together for a meal around the fire, with music and often stories. As the night ends, they all go to bed at the same time.

The amazing part about their lifestyle is not the family atmosphere, even though that is commendable. It is the life expectancy of the Bedouin shepherd: one hundred years. That's right! That is almost thirty years longer than the average life expectancy of Americans.

---

22 "The Bedouin Culture." Israel, Land of Creation. n.d. Web. January 15, 2015.

Why is their life expectancy so much longer? Their extremely low-stress lifestyle. Apparently the Israeli government was curious about the longevity of the shepherds as well, and they are the ones who discovered it was because of the very limited amount of stress in Bedouin lives. Frazee speaks about how these people just live this life, and how perhaps neither you nor I live such a simple stress-free life. He also notes the Bible does not speak about living like this because the people of the Bible would have just lived it; they would not have needed instruction on how to live that way. As very privileged people, Frazee suggests we need to learn how to reduce the stresses of life and work towards getting back to basics.[23]

I could not agree more. Not only should we as a people get back to the basics of just living life, but more importantly, we can do it. In fact, David, in Psalm 23, reminds us that living life free of stress is definitely possible if we allow the Shepherd to lead us.

SCRIPTURE REFLECTION: PSALM 23:1–6 KJV

> The LORD is my shepherd; I shall not want. He maketh me to lie down in green pastures: he leadeth me beside the still waters. He restoreth my soul: he leadeth me in the paths of righteousness for his name's sake. Yea, though I walk through the valley of the shadow of death, I will fear no evil: for thou art with me; thy rod and thy staff they comfort me. Thou preparest a table before me in the presence of mine enemies: thou anointest my head with oil; my cup runneth over. Surely goodness and mercy shall follow me all the days of my life: and I will dwell in the house of the LORD forever.

---

[23] "The Secret of the Bedouin shepherd: The Solution Is Not More of the Same." The Written Word. June 3, 2008. Web. January 17, 2015.

THE DEVOTIONAL

It was a Friday night, family night at the Stewart household. I was sitting at the dining room table, working to complete my manuscript for this book. Alexandria (Alex), a sophomore in college, sat next to me as I was writing. She looked at me with a look a father could not possibly deny. She needed online assistance to complete her financial aid application for the next school year. For some unknown reason, she was unable to successfully solicit the help of her sister, Mikaela. (Mikaela is the family's computer whiz.)

Together, Alex and I went through each question one by one, line by line, and section by section. As we were going through, it occurred to me that even though Alex was a second-year college student, she still needed some guidance. There was still somewhat of a dependence upon me and her mom. She was independent enough to live on her own on the college campus, but there were still some things only her father and mother could provide.

Here's another thing I discovered while completing this exercise: I enjoyed having her depend on my help!

I came away from that experience reminded that we, too, remain dependent upon God, our Father. It does not matter how long we have been Christians, how many degrees we have acquired, or how long we have served in various church capacities; we are still dependent upon God as our Father.

Not only are we eternally dependent upon the Lord, but the Lord is pleased when we express our dependence upon Him. The Proverb writer reminds us to "trust in the Lord with all thine heart; and lean not unto thine own understanding. In all thy ways acknowledge him, and he shall direct thy paths" (3:5–6). When we trust in the Lord unreservedly, we are indeed expressing our reliance upon His ability to keep us in all our ways. As an infant depends upon his or her parents for protection, food, shelter, and relationship, so does the Christian depend upon the Lord, the Good Shepherd. And when this happens, the Lord is pleased!

Psalm 23 is an exposition of how it is that we should depend upon the living Lord, who wants to care for us in the same way a shepherd cares for his sheep. There is no question in my mind that this psalm is one of the best-loved single passages in the Old Testament. David shares with us why this psalm continues to speak to the relevance trusting and depending on God.

JESUS IS OUR PROVIDER

When I hear the word *provider*, I think of words such as *supplier*, *giver*, *source*, or even *breadwinner*. Jesus is our provider. He is the supplier of our every need. He is the source of our ability to breathe. Jesus Christ is the giver of life itself. Psalm 23 was written to remind us that the Lord is our provider—and oh, how He provides for us!

The psalmist says, "The Lord is my shepherd." Nobody else but the Lord is my Shepherd. Brothers and sisters, we must be sure about the identity of Jesus. At Mt. Olive Baptist Church, where I currently serve as senior pastor, many people attend the church during the week for various ministry opportunities. Because of security measures, when the main entrance doors are locked, persons wishing to enter the building must ring the doorbell and announce their identity before they are allowed entrance. The church secretary will not allow entrance if they refuse to answer the question, "Who is it?" David lets us know immediately that it is the Lord who is his Shepherd. There is no question concerning the Lord's identity.

Notice how he makes it personal. He says that the Lord is "my" Shepherd. The Psalter witnesses to the intimacy of David's relationship with the Lord. I have discovered that when a Christian has a genuine relationship with the Lord, as a sheep has with his Shepherd, that person is confident beyond measure that the Lord indeed is "*my* shepherd."

For David to call God Shepherd means that God is his King, his Savior, and the One who meets all of his needs. And because God is our Shepherd, we shall not want for anything. Everything we need will be provided by the divine hand of God. Everything!

I received a call from a friend who was having a frustrating day, resulting from an issue of moving into another home. It seemed she could not secure a good leasing agreement. I shared with her my thoughts, and we prayed over the phone. I told her, "The Lord will take care of you."

A few days later, she called back with greater frustrations. Nothing was working out. She had exhausted every avenue in terms of finding a suitable place for her and her family. I asked if she had checked with church members; she said yes. I asked if she had checked with her beautician; she said yes. She had secured a licensed real estate agent to assist her, and that strategy wasn't working either. I gave her a couple of phone numbers from my research in the area.

Well, a few days later, she texted me, still frustrated because of no progress in finding a place to live. But this time, I did not respond to the text. I simply prayed this prayer: "Lord, you promised that you would not leave us nor forsake us. One of your children needs shelter for her and her family. Please provide in your time. Amen." I am sure there were prayers going up on her side of the phone as well.

The next day, I received a text stating that she had made a cash deposit on a beautiful home, which had more room and amenities than the other house she had wanted. Glory to God!

You see, because the Lord is our Shepherd, we shall not want for anything. Do you get that? Because the Lord is our Shepherd, everything we need will be provided by His hand. How will this happen?

The shepherd gives rest to His sheep. "He makes me to lie down in green pastures." We are living in times when everyone seems to be in a hurry. I went through the drive-through window at McDonalds not too long ago and discovered that they had added yet another drive-through telecom system to service even more hurrying customers.

In our hurried life, God desires our rest. The Sabbath was instituted, in part, to guarantee this. If we do not follow His pattern,

He may even enforce rest upon us. I can personally attest to the fact that God will place you under arrest in order to give you rest.

But notice that the place of rest is "green pastures." God wants His children resting in places of peace, tranquility, and nourishment. God does not want us living rushed lives or lazy lives, but rested lives.

In today's world, we are so goal-oriented and hurried that we feel guilty when we rest. We say things like, "I'm sorry, I overslept," as if sleeping is a bad thing. Some people brag about how little sleep they need in order to function. Perhaps that might explain why some of us are so easily irritated by others on Sunday mornings at church. Quite frankly, some of us would be less irritable during the day if we got more rest during the night.

The body needs rest. The mind needs rest. Jesus promises, "Come to me, all you who are weary and burdened, and I will give you rest. Take my yoke upon you and learn from me, for I am gentle and humble in heart, and you will find rest for your souls. For my yoke is easy and my burden is light" (Matt. 11:28–30). When God rests us, there is no guilt!

JESUS IS OUR PROTECTOR

Not only does the Lord provide for us, but David reminds us that He also protects us. You see, the "paths of righteousness" do not protect us from valley experiences, but the Lord leads us *through* the valley experiences, such as depression, downheartedness, and despair.

We have the presence of the Good Shepherd. I remember coming home from college as a freshman during the Christmas break. My brother Alvin and I went out to a Christmas or New Year's Eve party together (I can't remember which). Alvin was a senior in high school. He was also a basketball, football, powerlifting, and track standout. He was massively and athletically framed.

While I was at the party, a guy wanted to fight me over something that had happened back in high school. I did not wish to fight this guy. I was not afraid of him beating me down, but I was afraid of what my mother Annie Mae would do to me if I got in trouble and, as a result, got expelled from college. All night long this fella confronted me, trying to get me outside to fight. I simply walked away to the other side of the room to enjoy the music and the fellowship of friends.

Somehow or another, Alvin found out this person was harassing me. Alvin quickly made his way over to where a crowd of bystanders was beginning to form, and he calmly stood next to me. I do not recall Alvin saying one word to the guy; he just stood there looking ready to rumble. The man looked at Alvin, all of two hundred pounds of muscle, and it was as if he were suddenly looking into the eyes of the Incredible Hulk. He hurriedly backed up several steps.

For the balance of the evening, I was able to enjoy myself because I knew that my brother's presence was all I needed. Likewise, when God sent His people from Egypt to the Promised Land, He gave them one absolute guarantee: "My Presence will go with you, and I will give you rest" (Ex. 33:14). Many centuries later, we can still depend on this promise!

A Bedouin shepherd tending his sheep

In verse 5, David takes off the coat of a shepherd and puts on the apron of a host. A good host would attend to the needs of his guests, so David reminds us that the Lord, who is the Good Shepherd, will also provide for us by treating us as a special guest when we depend upon Him.

The Lord, as a Host, will do three things for us:

The Lord blesses *us in the midst of our enemies.* David said He prepares a table of blessings in the very presence of those who seek to do us harm. God never ceases to amaze me with how He continues to show favor to His children in the face of their enemies. This is not something we should boast about. We should be humbled by this fact. It is a humbling experience that God would bless me with favor when I am not deserving of the blessing. I have made many mistakes, both privately and publicly, and right when my enemies thought it was over for me, God gave me another chance. If God is for us, who can be against us? (Rom. 8:31).

The Lord encourages *us in the midst of our enemies.* It was the custom of a loving host to provide oil for the head of his honored guest, to refresh him after his travels. Thus David added, "You anoint my head with oil," speaking of the Lord's ministry to revive our hearts, especially when we are surrounded by those who threaten our existence. At Mt. Olive Baptist Church, I practice putting anointing oil on the foreheads of those who come forward for prayer. There is no power or supernatural anointing in the oil itself; the power is in what it symbolizes (James 5:14). It symbolizes God's power. It symbolizes God's approval. It symbolizes God's encouragement. It symbolizes God's protection (1 Sam. 10:1; Ps. 89:20). Thus, when I anoint the foreheads of the members of Mt. Olive, I am doing it to remind the people that it is God who gives you power, encouragement, healing, protection, and refreshment for His service. He is the Good Shepherd who anoints our heads with oil!

Surely goodness and mercy will follow me all the days of my life. David came to this conclusion even when he found himself in life-threatening situations. Through thick and thin, in every extremity of life, God's blessings were chasing David. No matter where David went, goodness and mercy was not far away. To know that goodness and mercy will always follow us around, no matter what happens, is splendid news.

I am from a rather large family. I love all my siblings. But as a little fella, probably around the age of five years old, I was enamored by the personhood of my older brother Tommie Stewart. When other little boys wanted to be like James Brown, Rifle Man, or Superman, I wanted to be like my brother Tommie.

Tommie was unflappable and hip to me. Whenever he was around, I literally followed him everywhere. If he was watching TV in the living room, I would figure out how to sit next to him and watch TV. If he got up and went to the kitchen during a commercial, I would get up and follow him to the kitchen. If he went to the bathroom, I would get up and try to go too.

He did not take issue with me when I followed him to the living room to watch TV. He had no issue with me following him to the kitchen. However, he did not like it when I followed him to the bathroom. But back then, we did not have locks on the restroom doors, so he could not prevent me from coming in while he was on the toilet.

One time, he warned me to leave the bathroom, but I refused to leave him in privacy. In fact, I remember teasing him that I would leave the bathroom door open so that all our company could see him using the toilet. As I left the door open and ran down the hallway, Tommie took off one of his shoes and threw it at me. Before I could get out of the line of fire, the airborne shoe hit me atop my head, causing me to fall forward and bump my head against the hallway wall.

I cried the entire day—not because it hurt that bad, but because of the embarrassment of being beat down by an airborne shoe! That was the last time I followed Tommie around. The good news for Christians is grace and mercy will *always* follow us around all the days of our lives!

This is what it means to depend totally upon God. God wants us to depend upon Him. When we depend totally upon God, we are totally independent of this world. When we find our identity and our security in Him, we are free to deal with life and not cave in to life. The Lord is our Shepherd!

For Further Discussion and Reflection:

1. What do Jesus and shepherds have in common?
2. How has the Lord provided for you other than food, clothes, and shelter?
3. Name three ways the Lord has protected you.
4. Why is it important to the Shepherd to ensure His sheep are well rested?
5. What significance is the oil to the Shepherd when caring for His sheep?

Chapter 17

Don't You Worry About a Thing—A Day of Sabbath

Day 14, Wednesday, September 9, 2009: Retreat Day, Back to the Mount of Olives, Gethsemane, Riding a Camel, Dinner in Bethlehem

Excursion Background

"This is it!" That is exactly what I said to myself as I opened my eyes from a great sleep in Jerusalem. This would be my last full day in the land of Jesus. Pat and Jim, our spiritual advisor and trip coordinator respectively, had scheduled this day as a retreat day. We could spend it doing what we wanted to do. Pat and Jim did not want us feeling hurried by having to stick to a timed agenda. It was a "no worry" day for us.

Some of the team went shopping for gifts to take back home. Some went visiting sites not on our daily agenda, such as Bethany. Some spent the day hanging around the hotel. I decided that I would do a variety of things, but restful things. I returned to the Mount of Olives and Gethsemane to spend time praying. I also did some light shopping in the Old City. I went over the Jericho road and took some pictures. A couple of pilgrims and I walked to the Upper Room on Mount Zion and reflected on the Last Supper.

I ended up also riding a camel for the first time in my life. I think the camel was partly in protest mode due to the heavy load he had to carry. It was, however, a very enjoyable experience.

Well, that is how I elected to spend part of my retreat day, my no-worry day, my Sabbath day!

Steven Kurtz, Major's roommate, kneeling in Lazarus's tomb on his day of retreat

The word *sabbath* means "to rest from labor." It is first mentioned as having been instituted in Paradise, when man was in innocence (Gen. 2:2). The Sabbath was made for us as a day of rest and refreshment for the body and of blessing to the soul. It is next referred to in connection with the gift of manna to the children of Israel in the wilderness (Exod. 16:23). Afterward, when the law was given from Sinai, the people were solemnly charged to "remember the Sabbath day, to keep it holy" (Exod. 20:11). In Mosaic law, very strict regulations existed with regard to what people could and could not do on the Sabbath (Exod. 35:2–3; Lev. 23:3; Lev. 26:34).

THE BLESSING AND BEAUTY OF RESTING

"Sabbath time can be a revolutionary challenge to the violence of overwork, mindless accumulation, and the endless multiplication of desires, responsibilities, and accomplishments. Sabbath is a way of being in a time where we remember who we are, remember what we know, and taste the gifts of spirit and eternity," writes ordained minister, therapist, and best-selling author Wayne Muller.[24]

Jews, Christians, and Muslims honor the need to create a sanctuary in time for worship, prayer, devotion, and thanks to God. Muller challenges us to take a Sabbath day of rest, to set aside a Sabbath afternoon for silence, and to create Sabbath moments in our hectic weekday schedules. He calls for a time of stillness and repose, a time for rejoicing in the goodness and holiness of life, and a time to surrender to the mystery of not-knowing.

Muller's book was required reading for our preparation for the spiritual journey to the Holy Land. I highly recommend this book for any Christian, regardless of one's point of progress in one's walk with Christ. It is good reading that will challenge traditional Sabbath-day views.

For instance, in the chapter "The Joy of Rest," Muller brings out that we as a people are so hurried in life that we do not realize how tired we are until we go away on vacation or a retreat. This insight was particularly true in my case during my stay in Israel. I felt rather guilty for sleeping and resting while some of the pilgrims visited other sites not on our agenda. I remember how much I struggled when a few pilgrims decided to spend a part of their retreat day in Bethany, the place where Lazarus was raised from the dead. I wanted to tag along because it is one of my favorite preaching passages. However, my body was begging for rest and renewal on that day. Rest and renewal won out over Lazarus.

---

[24] Wayne Muller. "Sabbath, Finding Rest, Renewal, and Delight in Our Busy Lives." (Bantam Books, New York, 2000),24

I am particularly impressed with how Muller unveils Jesus as being very concerned about rest as well. When we think of Jesus, we usually think of Him teaching, healing, or being accosted by hordes of the sick or the possessed who sought His touch. However, Jesus would often send people away or disappear without warning, dismissing those in need with neither excuse nor explanation, and retreating to a place of rest. Jesus did not wait until everyone had been adequately cared for, until all who sought Him were healed. He did not ask permission to go, nor did He leave anyone behind "on call" or even let His disciples know where He was going.

Jesus obeyed a deeper rhythm. When the moment for rest came, the time for healing was over. He would stop, return to a quiet place, and pray or rest.[25]

Matthew 14:23 says, "And when he had sent the multitudes away, he went up into a mountain apart to pray: and when the evening was come, he was there alone" (KJV).

Luke 5:15–16 says, "But so much the more went there a fame abroad of him: and great multitudes came together to hear, and to be healed by him of their infirmities. And he withdrew himself into the wilderness and prayed" (KJV).

Mark 1:32–36 says, "And at even, when the sun did set, they brought unto him all that were diseased, and them that were possessed with devils. And all the city was gathered together at the door. And he healed many that were sick of divers diseases, and cast out many devils; and suffered not the devils to speak, because they knew him. And in the morning, rising up a great while before day, he went out, and departed into a solitary place, and there prayed. And Simon and they that were with him followed after him" (KJV).

Thus, if taking time to repose, renew, restore, refresh, and regenerate was practiced by Jesus, then we should also practice resting or Sabbath. We should regularly practice setting aside time in

---

25   Wayne Muller. "Sabbath, Finding Rest, Renewal, and Delight in Our Busy Lives" (Bantam Books, New York, 2000),24

which we allow the cares and concerns of this world to fall naturally to the wayside. Then we can delight in being alive and giving thanks for the blessings we may have missed while we were preoccupied with our work.

SCRIPTURE REFLECTION: MATTHEW 6:25–34 KJV

Therefore I say unto you, Take no thought for your life, what ye shall eat, or what ye shall drink; nor yet for your body, what ye shall put on. Is not the life more than meat, and the body than raiment? Behold the fowls of the air: for they sow not, neither do they reap, nor gather into barns; yet your heavenly Father feedeth them. Are ye not much better than they? Which of you by taking thought can add one cubit unto his stature? And why take ye thought for raiment? Consider the lilies of the field, how they grow; they toil not, neither do they spin: And yet I say unto you, That even Solomon in all his glory was not arrayed like one of these. Wherefore, if God so clothe the grass of the field, which today is, and tomorrow is cast into the oven, shall he not much more clothe you, O ye of little faith? Therefore take no thought, saying, What shall we eat? or, What shall we drink? or, Wherewithal shall we be clothed? (For after all these things do the Gentiles seek:) for your heavenly Father knoweth that ye have need of all these things. But seek ye first the kingdom of God, and his righteousness; and all these things shall be added unto you. Take therefore no thought for the morrow: for the morrow shall take thought for the things of itself. Sufficient unto the day is the evil thereof.

THE DEVOTIONAL

One of my favorite performers of all time, Stevie Wonder, wrote a hit single in 1973 called "Don't You Worry 'bout a Thing." It was a very popular song among various age and ethnic groups. In fact, the song climbed the charts to the number 2 spot on the R&B chart. The song's lyrics convey a positive message, focusing on taking things in one's stride and accentuating the positive. No matter what is going on in one's life, there is no need to worry to a fault, because someone dependable is standing by to help you.

Guess what, child of God? We have Someone dependable standing by us to help in times of worry and fear! What is it that has you worried? What's the source of your anxiety? Are you listening to the prophets of doom, hearing only about what's wrong? Until you can *express* your worries and fears, you can't *expel* your worries and fears. Putting your worries into words will help to disrobe and unveil them. When they are disrobed and unveiled, they become weak, naked, and harmless. You see, God did not give the Christian a spirit of fear (2 Tim. 1:7).

The movie *The Wizard of Oz* starts out with a tornado slashing through Kansas. Dorothy and her dog, Toto, are taken away in their house to the magical land of Oz. Trying to find their way back to Kansas, they follow the Yellow Brick Road toward the Emerald City to meet the Wizard called Oz to help them with their problem.

On their way, they meet a Scarecrow who needs a brain, a Tin Man who needs a heart, and a Cowardly Lion who wants courage. Convincing Dorothy and her three friends that he is the only person capable of solving their problems, the Wizard asks the group to bring him the broom of the Wicked Witch of the West to earn his help.

When Dorothy and her friends finally accomplish all that Oz demands of them, Oz still gives them a hard time. Eventually, the curtains behind him are pulled back, and it is revealed that Oz is actually a powerless fake. Once the curtains are pulled back, he is literally exposed.

Likewise, you must pull back the curtain and expose your worries and your fears. The apostle Paul gives us insight on how to make this happen when he says, "Don't worry about anything; instead, pray about everything. Tell God what you need, and thank him for all he has done. Then you will experience God's peace, which exceeds anything we can understand. His peace will guard your hearts and minds as you live in Christ Jesus" (Phil. 4:6–7 NLT). When you expose your worries and fears through prayer, you will discover that your worries and fears are weak and faint compared to God's power and peace!

*Major wearing a paper yamakah. Time to pray
at the Wailing Wall in Jerusalem.*

WHY YOU SHOULD NOT WORRY

"Therefore I say unto you, Take no thought for your life" (v. 25). The word *therefore* is a bridge word, tying this section to the preceding section. Someone said that when we see the word *therefore*, we should look back a few verses to see what it is *there for* us to see.

Jesus is emphasizing that, having decided to serve one Master, it follows that we perform the duties of obedience. As servants, we look to our Master for His care and trust Him for our well-being. This call to trust God is an answer to the human tendency to worry. We find it easier to feel secure with things that we can control. When something is beyond our control, we worry. But when we find greater security in God, we can trust Him for our needs. Christ calls us to give up our limited securities for the greater security in Him.

Jesus wants us to know that worrying is not good. It's not good because it is damaging to our health. It's not good because it interferes with us getting things done in life. You cannot be productive when your mind is on something over which you have no control. Worrying is not good because it negatively affects how you treat people around you. We tend to become easily irritable when we are worried. We sometimes become rude and short with people. The most important reason we should not worry is because it reduces our ability to trust God.

It should be noted that worry is not the same as being concerned. We should be a concerned people. We ought to be concerned about the issues of life, but we ought not be worried about the issues of life. The difference between worry and genuine concern is that worry immobilizes you, but concern moves you to action. For instance, if you are experiencing health issues, *worrying* will cause you to procrastinate about going to see your doctor. However, when you are *concerned* about your health, you will immediately call and make an appointment to find out what's going on with your body.

"Take therefore no thought for the morrow" (v. 34). Notice that Matthew encourages us not to worry about tomorrow. It is one thing to worry about today, but something more devastating when worrying about tomorrow. Worrying about tomorrow is a waste of time and energy. We should be mindful to plan for tomorrow, but should not worry about tomorrow.

Planning for tomorrow has to do with thinking ahead with the intent of accomplishing a goal. It has to do with scheduling and strategizing your steps of action to achieve your goals. Careful planning involves trusting God for ultimate guidance. The purpose of planning is to alleviate worry as much as possible. Typically, the more we prayerfully plan, the less we worry.

On the other hand, when people worry, they tend to allow their fears to immobilize them from taking action to help realize their goals and dreams. They usually become more consumed by their fears and then refuse to act on their faith in God to resolve their issue. They refuse to pray for guidance and direction. This is a devastating and unfortunate state because worrying about tomorrow is only adding a load of burdens on what you are attempting to accomplish today.

It must be noted that careful and prayerful plans will not alleviate the troubles and problems of tomorrow. Planning will not erase trials and tribulations. However, worrying will incapacitate our strength for dealing with those trials and tribulations. George MacDonald put it this way: "No man ever sank under the burden of the day. It is when tomorrow's burden is added to the burden of today, that the weight is more than a man can bear."[26]

For Further Discussion and Reflection:

1. Have you ever experienced a situation in which you worried about something and it negatively affected you? What was it?
2. To you, what does it mean to worry?
3. How does worry reveal wrong priorities in life?
4. How does worry show a lack of trust in God?
5. What are some ways in which we can seek Jesus when tempted to worry?

---

[26] Kent R. Hughes. "Preaching the Word - The Sermon on the Mount: The Message of the Kingdom. (Crossway Books, Wheaton, IL 2001), 219.

Chapter 18

CONCLUDING THOUGHTS—
THE END IS NOT HERE

It was a great day for me. After years of writing and rewriting the Israel manuscript, I was now finished. Five years of intermittently picking up the pen and writing about the growth and the lessons learned while walking where Jesus walked were now complete. I felt a profound joy for having obediently fulfilled this charge to write. The feeling was like graduating from high school or college all over again.

Imagine the surprise I felt when a trusted advisor called me upon completing the first phase of editing, to tell me something could be missing from the manuscript. At the time, I thought surely everything I had intended to write was in there. So I replied, "Missing?"

"Well," said my advisor, "on Thursday, August 27, you took me as the reader on a journey following Jesus. You took me to Capernaum, the Mount of Beatitudes, the Sea of Galilee, Nazareth, and Banias. Then on Friday, September 4, you took me to Jerusalem, where I experienced being at the Mount of Olives, Gethsemane, Bethlehem, the Garden Tomb, and the Dead Sea. But you never seemed to take me, the reader, back home. At the end of your journey, you got on a plane and returned. You left me, the reader, on the journey. You did not take me home with afterthoughts or debriefing from the pilgrimage."

At first, I was speechless. I was driving when the call came. I politely expressed my surprise and said I would take the observation into consideration.

Mentally, I began to review the manuscript, fresh in my mind as if the pilgrimage were yesterday. Then it hit me: it was fresh because the impact of the experience had never ended. Especially each time I picked up my proverbial pen, the spiritual journey was still in process! *Physically*, I had returned from walking in the land of Jesus, but *spiritually*, the experience continued to impact my life.

I am still on the journey. I am no longer in Jerusalem, but I am still on the journey. As long as you continue to seek after the things of God, you never finish the journey. That is how life-changing this experience is: you never finish the journey.

Finally, my response was this: "The journey is not intended to end. It continues no matter where you are, no matter where you go. There are no expiration dates attached to the journey. There are no renewal dates on it. The journey continues."

It is my greatest desire that each time you pick up this book and reflect on the various places where Jesus walked, a new spiritual experience will take place in your life. I pray that your desire to grow spiritually will not end here.

One of my favorite Scripture passages I have committed to memory is Proverbs 3:5–6: "Trust in the Lord with all thine heart, and lean not unto thine own understanding. In all, thy ways acknowledge him, and he shall direct thy paths" (KJV). I have preached it, I have studied it in seminary, and I have taught many Bible study lessons on this portion of Scripture.

However, one day these verses took on an entirely different meaning for me. It was the same passage and the same interpretation, but it now had a richer meaning. I had been involved in a car accident, and my car was banged up quite a bit. So was I, mentally, as it turned out. While waiting for the state trooper to come and fill out an accident report, I became nervous about what to expect from him. When he arrived, he asked me for my driver's license, vehicle registration, and proof of insurance.

I found my license and gave it to him. I found the vehicle registration and gave it to him. But I could not find proof of insurance. Now I was very nervous.

The state trooper agreed to talk to the other people who were involved in the accident, to give me a chance to find my insurance papers. It was then that I began to pray Proverbs 3:5–6. This was the only verse that came to my mind. But this time, as I quoted this very familiar verse, it was with a different tone. It was under the guise of an emergency. This was serious business of another sort. I needed the Lord to direct my path right now. I needed insurance papers in the most urgent way. I was not in the mood for receiving a citation for driving without insurance.

While I was yet praying this Scripture, the state trooper, who was a Sergeant, walked up and knocked on the window. My heartbeat increased, even beyond the rate it was beating from the initial effect of the crash. I was looking for the papers but was still empty-handed. The patient but serious-looking Sergeant stood there, waiting.

I lowered the window at his gesture. He asked for the insurance papers once more. I was about to give up and surrender to being cited for driving without insurance. I decided to look once more in the glove compartment. There it was, neatly folded underneath one final piece of paper. What a relief! "Thank you, Lord!" I whispered. Once again, the Lord showed Himself faithful. He directed my hands in the right place at the right time, and I found the papers. Proverbs 3:5–6 had taken on a brand-new meaning to me.

Before the crash, this was just another passage I had committed to memory and a homework assignment from seminary. After the crash, it has become my lifeline. It is my "way out of no way" passage. These two verses meant more to me that day than at any time in the past.

In the same way, as you continue to walk in the footsteps of Jesus, your journey will not end but will, I hope, mean something more important to you with each experience in life. Each time you visit, through meditation, the Garden Tomb of Jesus, I pray that the resurrection power of Jesus becomes more evident in your life as you continue to live for the Lord. As you walk in His footsteps, I pray that you walk with confidence and encouragement atop the circumstances that unpredictable sea storms tend to bring. My desire is that you will strive to live for the Lord. I pray that Christian living will always be your goal in life.

The pilgrims of 2009

Our group gathered a few weeks after our return from Jerusalem to reflect upon, celebrate, and bring closure to our pilgrimage. It was evident that significant life-changing, renewing, refreshing, and revitalizing events had been experienced by all. It turned out to be a time of celebrating the newness and extension of life and ministry and not just closure to our pilgrimage.

Whenever you feel the need to draw closer to Christ, it is my prayer that this book will be a resource to help renew, refresh, and revitalize you on your journey. *Walking in His Footsteps*, I pray, will be a book you continually use throughout your study, devotion, or meditation time on the Word of God. The end is not here—the journey continues!

AFTERWORD

Let me begin by thanking God for leading Dr. Major A. Stewart to write this devotional book, *Walking in His Footsteps*. To my knowledge, there have been many books written on devotions but never one like this one. The book is written from a personal experience, and to me that makes it special.

Dr. Stewart reminds me of three of my favorite bible characters: Joseph, a man of integrity; Joshua, a man of courage; and Daniel, a man of great faith. To me, the author is all three in one.

After a careful examination of eighteen chapters written by Dr. Stewart, I am certain that he has put in many hours of prayer, study, and work to complete them. I am also confident that there is more yet to come from this great author.

Let me close by saying I believe that, when this book is published and the church community reads it, it will become a best seller. So keep up the good work, God bless, and keep writing.

Sincerely,

Rev. Dr. Roosevelt Austin Sr.
Pastor Emeritus
Zion Missionary Baptist Church
Saginaw, Michigan

Appendix

Pilgrim Team 2009

1. Carol Bastin—Emmaus, PA
2. David Bryant Jr.—Chicago, IL
3. Pam Cook—Paoli, IN
4. Cynthia Davis—Memphis, TN
5. Linda Dulin—Sidney, OH
6. Jim Eller (trip coordinator)—Englewood, OH
7. Pat Eller (spiritual advisor)—Englewood, OH
8. Tim Forbess—Dayton, OH
9. Curnell Graham—Cincinnati, OH
10. Kimberly Hall—Timonium, MD
11. Katie Hayes—Waynesfield, OH
12. Larry Karow—Fort Thomas, KY
13. Kurt King—Cincinnati, OH
14. Steven Kurtz—Daphne, AL
15. Brian Maguire—Beavercreek, OH
16. Scott Miller—Cincinnati, OH
17. Mary Nesmith—Boynton Beach, FL
18. J. W. Park—Germantown, MD
19. Steve Putka—Worthington, OH
20. Tim Reeves—West Liberty, OH
21. Tammy Jo Reiser—West Chester, OH
22. Major A. Stewart—Flint, MI

ABOUT THE AUTHOR

Reverend Dr. Major A. Stewart is a man after the heart of God for the people of God. He is committed to the high standards the Lord has set before him to cause the people to rise up, grow in grace and the knowledge of the Lord giving Him all the Glory for the power to possess the inheritance of the Kingdom. (2 Peter 3:18; Matthew 28:18 & Deuteronomy 10:11) Dr. Stewart leads with clear passion, energetic vitality and unconditional love; the mandate to follow the standard of the apostles' teaching to enrich the lives of the saints spiritually and physically to witness the signs and wonders of God. (Act 2:42-44)

Rev. Dr. Major A. Stewart, a native of Muskegon, Michigan, accepted God's call to the ministry of Jesus Christ in 1986. He was first licensed at Golden Leaf Missionary Baptist Church (now Promise Tabernacle Baptist Church) in Flint, Michigan. Later, after employer relocation, Pastor Stewart was ordained in December 1995 at St. Paul Missionary Baptist Church in Oxnard, California. Pastor Stewart, is now, in his twenty-ninth year of preaching the Gospel. He left a legacy for Christian Education, as Senior Pastor for ten years, at Gethsemane Baptist Church prior to the Lord's reassignment to Mount Olive Missionary Baptist Church where he serves currently as Senior Pastor.

Dr. Stewart is actively involved in church leadership currently as a Vice Moderator in the Great Lakes District Baptist Association, taught at Michigan Theological Institue and is a Certified Instructor in the Great Lakes Congress of Christian Education and National

Baptist Congress of Christian Education. Yet, Dr. Stewart works to contribute toward his community as a member of the Flint Chapter of NAACP and Epsilon Eta Chapter of Alpha Phi Alpha Fraternity and Board Member of International Academy of Flint School. Given the gift of teaching, Dr. Stewart is a former adjunct part-time instructor at Concordia University, where he taught courses in accounting, business policy, and marketing management. He traveled to Turkey and Asia Minor (tracing the footsteps of the apostle Paul) in 2001; to Monrovia, Liberia, on a mission team in 2005; and to Israel with a United Theological Seminary pilgrimage team in 2009.

Dr. Stewart earned a bachelor's degree from Eastern Michigan University in accounting and finance, a master of business administration degree from California Lutheran University; a master of arts degree in Christian education from the Michigan Theological Seminary and a doctor of ministry degree from United Theological Seminary, as well as, completed the Church Management Certificate program at Villanova University. He has a passion and experience in congregational mission development.

Publications:

1. *Key Elements of an Effective Church Administration Strategy, the African American Lectionary, the Dialogue Corner, Church Enrichment 2013.*
2. Dissertation: *Leading the Black Church in the 21ˢᵗ Century in Achieving its Biblical Purpose through Developing Written Policies and Procedures*, United Theological Seminary, Dayton, Ohio, 2004.
3. *Walking in His Footsteps, A Devotional Journey in the Land of Jesus.*

Rev. Dr. Stewart is married to Carla Brooks-Stewart, and they are parents of three daughters: Alexandria Janine, Mikaela Ann, and Karissa Danielle.

Printed in the United States
By Bookmasters